SpringerBriefs in Computer Science

Series Editors

Stan Zdonik
Peng Ning
Shashi Shekhar
Jonathan Katz
Xindong Wu
Lakhmi C. Jain
David Padua
Xuemin Shen
Borko Furht
V. S. Subrahmanian
Martial Hebert
Katsushi Ikeuchi
Bruno Siciliano

For further volumes:
http://www.springer.com/series/10028

Il-Chul Moon · Kathleen M. Carley
Tag Gon Kim

Modeling and Simulating Command and Control

For Organizations Under Extreme Situations

 Springer

Il-Chul Moon
Department of Industrial
  and Systems Engineering
KAIST
Yuseong-gu, Daejeon
Republic of South Korea

Tag Gon Kim
Department of Electrical Engineering
KAIST
Yuseong-gu, Daejeon
Republic of South Korea

Kathleen M. Carley
Institute for Software Research
  International, SCS
Carnegie Mellon University
Pittsburgh, PA
USA

ISSN 2191-5768   ISSN 2191-5776 (electronic)
ISBN 978-1-4471-5036-7   ISBN 978-1-4471-5037-4 (eBook)
DOI 10.1007/978-1-4471-5037-4
Springer London Heidelberg New York Dordrecht

Library of Congress Control Number: 2013933302

Printed on acid-free paper

Springer is part of Springer Science+Business Media (www.springer.com)

Preface

This short book is a collection of my major researches and projects in the field of command and control from 2004 to 2012. I started my research on the command and control from 2004 at Center for Computational Analysis on Social and Organizational Systems (CASOS), Carnegie Mellon University. My first research of command and control with my advisor, Prof. Kathleen M. Carley, was analyzing the squad team performance in a first-person-shooting game, America's Army. At that time, the US Army was interested in utilizing the game to train soldiers before their deployments. Therefore, measuring how much players gained knowledge about squad teamwork was an important task. My analysis showed pros and cons of using the game as a training simulator. The game did improve players' communication behaviors that imply a better command and control at the squad level. However, some players were not serious in playing the game, and sometimes, the players just throw grenades in front of them to take out many enemies including themselves. This unrealistic behavior gave me fundamental questions: can the modeling and simulation regenerate critical real-world situations? Given that many existing studies utilize the models that are rarely validated, this question of validity still follows my researches and projects.

After my initial research topic with the smallest military unit, I confronted more scenarios that involve larger units with diverse nature. For example, while working at CASOS, I analyzed the command and control of Brigade Combat Team (BCT), and the command and control of various terrorist organizations. These scenarios gained interests because the two organizations shared one common aspect. They have network structures that are not similar to the tree-like hierarchy. Though we formally represent the hierarchical organizational structure of the BCT, the scenarios of interests required dynamics inside of the structure, such as collaboration across branches. At the beginning, I tried to analyze the structure with network analyses, but I found out that the dynamics is difficult to be estimated with the network analyses alone. I needed to regenerate the dynamics, and I also required observing the dynamics in all the aspects with many replications. Subsequently, modeling and simulation became the only option that I can continue my research on command and control. Moreover, this usage of modeling and simulation is particularly called upon when analyzing the opponents. There were limited information and observation chances in the operation of the terror organizations, so understanding their dynamics necessarily required me to model them with limited knowledge. At this point, I still looked for a possible approach to validate my models. If my model were daily traffic in an urban area, I might be able to validate my model. However, my modeling domain was command and control in an extreme situation, so a dataset that is big enough to attempt the validation was far from the reach. Due to this context, I felt that modeling and simulation should not be the only approach in analyzing these extreme scenarios. Hence, I further studied and applied network mining and text mining techniques to problems at hand. However, these approaches are often difficult to be used in what-if scenario analyses that I should evaluate various strategies to support or attack the structure.

After receiving my doctoral degree in 2008, I came back to Korea to finish my military service. During my service, under Prof. Tag Gon Kim who is another co-author of this book, I was tasked to analyze the fleet naval air defense because Korea just obtained her first AEGIS destroyer. Acquiring the weapon system can be done by budget, but operating the system with human factors takes a long time of experience. Because the system requires a number of human interventions in its operation, the command and control of the destroyer and its fleet is critical in its operational performance. However, as acknowledged in the above, there would be marginal command and control experience unless we deploy the destroyer to diverse situations. Then, until we have gained enough experience and historic data, at least, I had to rely on modeling and simulating the naval air defense operation in the virtual environment. At this time, while I model the command and control, I tried to be more formal, explicit, and transparent. Unless I perform a validation study, this was the least guideline that I had to keep. I started using a formalism to describe my models unambiguously, and I continue to meticulously analyze the virtual experiment result with diverse statistical techniques.

My research has been driven by the practical demand as well as the academic endeavor. The practical demand is analyzing rarely observed scenarios in the intelligence and military field to produce insights that can be applied to the real world. The academic endeavor is performing the analysis with scientific discipline, such as results that can be reproduced by other scientists. I felt that it is very delicate to satisfy both objectives, but I also think that pursuing the objectives at the same time is doable. This book presents three case studies that I struggle to achieve both practicality and scientific rigor. The presented works are completed for now, but through my research, I hope to find a better way to analyze and contribute.

This book is supported by the Public welfare and safety research program through the National Research Foundation of Korea (NRF), (2012-0029881).

Daejeon, Republic of South Korea   Il-Chul Moon

Contents

Chapter 1
Introduction

Keywords Collective · Authority · Individual · Al Qaeda · Command and control structure · Organization · Hierarchy · Tree structure · Commander · Network · OODA loop · System · Network structure · Agent · Agency · ICCRTS · Social network analysis · Modeling and simulation · Soar · Dynamic network analysis · Meta-network · Organizational structure · Command and control · Management · Disaster management · Intelligence · Military

The true competence of an organization is revealed when it confronts hard times (Dynes and Tierney 1994). Hard times caused by terrorists (Stadler et al. 2005), wars (Sorokin 1942), and disasters (Barton 1963) test and divulge the strength of the organization as a collective, not just a collection of individuals. In the process of weathering these threats, the collective should organize its personnel and resources efficiently and robustly (Yuchtman and Seashore 1967; Oliver 1997; Gold et al. 2001). Let us imagine a town struck by a hurricane. The town authority should efficiently evacuate its population to a safe location. After the evacuation, the authority and dispatched disaster responders need to deliver the basic supports—such as food, medicine, and energy—to the evacuees (McEntire 2006). Over the course of the response, the authority and the outside organizations, such as federal response teams, should collaborate seamlessly by sharing information and allocating limited resources to critical positions. Furthermore, a hurricane might cause unexpected damage to key infrastructure, so disaster responders might have to improvise their activities, and enabling improvisation may require double-preparation of resources for estimated losses. Ultimately, the disaster will test the efficiency and robustness of the town leadership and the responders in an extreme situation. In the real world, the end story of such extreme situations occasionally shows some heroic actions by individuals as well as some systematic failures by a collective. Then, our question is how to design and assess the collective system to be prepared for such extremes.

We can find scenarios that are analogous to the above disaster management scenario from the military and intelligence fields. For instance, a naval air defense

I.-C. Moon et al., *Modeling and Simulating Command and Control*,
SpringerBriefs in Computer Science, DOI: 10.1007/978-1-4471-5037-4_1,
© Il-Chul Moon 2013

scenario (Karasakal 2008) from the military domain shares similar challenges in disaster management. The naval air defense is a defense mission of a fleet to counter incoming multiple antiship missiles. Warships of the fleet should coordinate the defense plan in this extremely urgent and risky situation. From the intelligence domain, a terrorist organization performing a mission might share common aspects. The mission should be executed in a timely manner and through collaboration with terrorists and terror organizations (Moon 2008). The mission's success lies in preparing the personnel, the resources, and information—all at the right place and at the right time.

This book provides three case studies modeling and simulating extreme scenarios in the military, intelligence, and disaster management domains. Since there are many facets of the scenarios, this book focuses mainly on the management aspects. Management includes organizing the collectives, allocating resources, and mitigating events through the decision-making process. These management activities are called "command and control" in the military and intelligence domains (Alberts and Hayes 2006; Berkowitz 1996). Additionally, some civilian domains, such as disaster management, also call the activities command and control (Rosen et al. 2002; Harrald 2006). We show that the scenarios in this book emphasize human decision making, and management frequently becomes the determinant of the organizational performance. For instance, our scenario and simulation-based experiment illustrate that naval air defense might be more successfully carried out by giving more time to human decision making instead of procuring a better weapons system. Similarly, we show how terrorists relocate and connect to other terrorists to prepare for a mission in a hostile environment.

1.1 Command and Control in Diverse Domains

"Command and control" is originally military terminology for managing military units and executing their operations. Below is one of its formal definitions (U.S. Joint Chiefs of Staff 1986):

> Command and control is the exercise of authority and direction by a properly designated commander over assigned forces in the accomplishment of the mission. Command and control functions are performed through an arrangement of personnel, equipment, communications, facilities, and procedures which are employed by a commander in planning, directing, coordinating, and controlling forces and operations in the accomplishment of the mission.

Given the definition, the military has a clear hierarchy in its formal structure, and the right exercise of the commanding authority is critical in enhancing the force efficiently to achieve its mission. Because of the hierarchy that should organize a collective effort, the commander is the key person in preparing and coordinating the organizational elements in his or her forces. Hence, the study of the command and control boils down to the question of how to assign key personnel, equipment, communications, and facilities to the forces, as well as how to link such organizational elements to efficiently achieve the goal. This question can be viewed as factors of structuring the organization and assigning roles in the process of the mission's execution. In the military, the commander exercises his or her sole authority of forces to answer these questions of organization.

From the perspective of exercising authority, the public administration has the same concept of the command and control (McGuire 2006; Comfort 2007). Similar to the clear hierarchy system of the military, the public administration has the hierarchy between the administration offices, such as local, state, and federal offices (Peters and Pierre 1998). One different aspect is the rank system that defines who the commander is at the scene; in other words, who has the proper authority to organize the key elements. For instance, in the traditional military, there is no doubt when pointing out the commanding officer, if all officers are accounted at the moment. On the other hand, civil offices might have a key person of authority on the ground, yet there might be no intuitive rank system to determine who exercises the authority and to what extent. Having said that, it is important to make known who is in charge and to what extent to allow for an efficient organization. Many disaster response cases illustrate that the lack of knowledge-sharing on the command and control structure and authority lead to the malfunction of the collective system.

In the intelligence domain, command and control can be either very strict or very flexible by case. For instance, a terrorist organization such as Al Qaeda has two faces of informal and formal command and control structure at the same time (Sageman 2004). It has been known that the top command and control structure of Al Qaeda follows a hierarchical structure similar to the military. The head structure selects targets and executes operations by following the authority of its leader. On the other hand, the mission execution structure of the terror organizations often becomes amorphous and flexible by the gray line of memberships, roles, and authorities. Still, every important moment of a terrorist mission needs to be guided by commanding personnel to lead the flexible collective to the strict mission objectives.

1.2 Research on Command and Control

Command and control has been a research topic that has lasted many generations because the paradigm of organizations, the used technologies, and the surrounding contexts have evolved over those generations. In the early days, researchers focused on qualitative aspects of command and control. For instance, traditional researchers argue, using *qualitative* argument, who should be a leader and why. On the contrary, recent studies on command and control focus on how to form a self-organized command and control network and how to measure the efficiency of such network *quantitatively*. We briefly review such efforts in this subsection.

1.2.1 Traditional Command and Control Research

Max Weber, a founding father of modern sociology, defined *organization* as an institution to control individuals in the interest of the organization leader's goals (Weber 1947). If we follow Weber's idea, an organization requires a system to control individuals, orienting them to the point at which their leader aims. Fundamentally, this control system was implemented as laws, practices, rules, manuals, and so on. Rarely is there a question of who was in charge and how to communicate with subordinates since the organization usually has a typical hierarchy that explicitly points to who the commander is and how the command will propagate, as opposed to researching the structural aspects of command and control. In other words, the organizational ranking and hierarchy seem to be equal to the structure of its command and control. Thus, an individual with higher social class commands and controls a number of individuals in the lower ranks. Furthermore, the controlled individual follows no more than one or two higher-ranking individuals, which naturally makes the command and control structure a *tree structure,* or a *hierarchy* (Brown 1978). This typical hierarchical structure and corresponding roles were granted, so the question was mainly asked how to fulfill the structure and the roles rather than about changing them.

Traditional research has concentrated on the good characteristics of the commander in an organization (Bass 1985; Yuki and Van Fleet 1982). Such characteristics are revealed through a number of real-world cases, and the case study is still the most common practice in studying the leadership of corporations, governments, and the military. For example, Builder et al. draw ten command concepts from six cases of real-world combat (Builder et al. 1999). The selected command concepts are important yet very qualitative, general concepts. For example, one of the command concepts dictates "a structuring of forces consistent with the battle tasks to be accomplished." Considering that the cases include the Second World War, Korean War, Vietnam War, and so on, we may assume that these past battle tasks and the past structuring of forces are unchanging and explicit in the given circumstances. This is quite different from the constantly changing operational environment that we have seen recently. Hence, there is a great difference in following the command concept in the static past battles and in the recent dynamic situations: Following the good command concept from past battles in the current battlefield is not an easy task.

Moreover, the heavy research on the theory of commander's role represents the very "commander-centric" perspective on command and control. This point is made by Alberts and Nissen, who compared and contrasted the commander-centric perspective to the network-centric perspective (Alberts and Nissen 2009). While the latter emphasizes the right composition and right structure of the forces, the former solely emphasizes the role of human decision-making elements at key positions in the structure. This sole emphasis on commanders might fit to the circumstance in which there are few differences between the structures of two opposing forces—which would not be applicable to recent extreme crises.

This conventional thought on the commander's role is also reflected in the famous command and control procedure called "OODA loop." An OODA loop is a loop of *observe*, *orient*, *decide*, and *act* stages in commanding and controlling a force (Brehmer 2005). As the loop implies, this is a feedback procedure for the commander of the forces. In engineering, this feedback procedure is analogous to a control system (Franklin et al. 2009). The operation of the control system is as follows: First, a controller anticipates the environmental uncertainty. Second, the controller decides the inputs to the controlled system in the uncertain environment to match the targeted output. Third, the controller reconfigures the inputs by observing the deviation between the actual output and the target output. Similar to this control system, commanders receive the situation report, and they redirect and configure their forces to accomplish the mission. Then, they devise the course of action of their forces to prepare for the *act* stage. Finally, the commander's forces execute the course of action, and the commander starts this procedure again with after-action reviews. Contemplating this process of control, we can identify that the OODA loop is based upon an assumption that commanders have near perfect authority and capability to control their forces. Nevertheless, we question whether the commanders really have full authority and capability to control their forces in the battlefield of this generation. Though commanders are formally given the authority to command, many battlefield elements interfere with each other, diverse branches cooperate at the same time, and some units may not be in the communication channel when they are needed.

1.2.2 Recent Command and Control Research

In 1950s and 1960s, researchers started on a potential command and control structure other than the hierarchical structure. This direction of research fundamentally rests on the assumption that an organization is not a mere collection of individuals to control (Simon 1964; Bittner 1965; March and Simon 1958): Once an organization is formed, the interactions among the agents (Perrow 1986; Eisenhardt 1989; Carley and Newell 1994), who are different from individuals by emphasizing their *agency*,[1] make the organization as more than the sum of individuals. This is very much analogical to the definition of a system in engineering, which defines *system* as a collection of components to achieve a goal that a single component cannot achieve (Blanchard and Fabrycky 2010; Suh 2005). To see the difference between the individuals and the agents, researchers investigated how the self-motivated behavior of agents influences other agents and how the influence

---

[1] We define *agency* as the capacity of individuals to act independently and make their own free choices. In the military, the individuals are soldiers who take orders from their commanders, so some may see that they do not have *agency*. However, the current trend of military doctrine emphasizes the self-motivated, the self-organizing, and the self-synchronized units; this trend facilitates soldiers to have *agency* to actively engage and cooperate in the situation in play.

effects achieving the organizational goal (Mohr 1973). Eventually, the concept of command and control in the recent trend has evolved to manage the interactions and the influences among the self-motivated and self-governing agents to achieve the mission objective. Dating back to the beginning of this structural study, for instance, Herbert Simon looked at structures such as all-channel, wheel, circle, and so on (Guetzkowm and Simon 1955). He quantitatively investigated the path length from one agent to another as a proxy measure to information-sharing between agents. Compared to the traditional command and control research, this study transforms the concept of the command and control from a methodology to *order* and *manage* the organization to a way to have *better coordination* to jointly achieve the mission. Another distinction from the traditional words is the usage of quantitative analyses on command and control. Previously, the quantitative analyses were heavily used to bolster the qualitative ideas, and the quantitative approaches are now used to identify new qualitative thoughts on command and control.

This trend of applying quantitative analyses to command and control has been mainly introduced by the International Command and Control Research Technology Symposium (ICCRTS) series (U.S. Department of Defense 2013). Among many quantitative analyses from the symposium, we recognize two most frequently utilized approaches: the social network analysis (Wasserman and Faust 1994) and the modeling and simulation analysis (Tolk 2012). *Social network analysis* is an approach to investigate the various characteristics of social structure, mainly represented as a graph structure (White et al. 1976). Social network analysis uses clustering algorithms, for instance, Newman clustering to find the cohesive group (Newman 2001), as well as property measures, such as degree centrality to measure the relative position of an entity on the structure (Friedkin 1991). When this analysis is applied, researchers identified the cohesive groups that might cover units from different branches. This heterogeneous group would not be formally represented in the conventional military system, yet they have close interactions when they face a situation. Then, the idea to improve the command and control is how to govern these eclectic units in a close working relationship by creating a *joint* command and control. Another application scenario is employing the social network analysis measures on assessing cognitive burdens and the information flow of command and control. If a commander has many subordinate units—which would suggest many links from the commander to the units—the commander may suffer from information overload in an actual situation. Such problems would compromise the performance of the command and control, and the problem should be resolved by reconfiguring the network; for example, assigning mid-class commanders to the commander to help in controlling the units.

The *modeling and simulation analysis* is a method to generate the expected situation virtually and walk through the virtual situation with models representing command and control and the units (Levchuk et al. 1996; Macal and North 2010; Daly and Tolk 2003). For example, a command post exercise (CPX) is a live simulation that imitates the command and control in the scenario of interests

(French and Hutchinson 2002). Through the live simulation, we can detect potential problems of command and control procedures and structures. While the live simulation provides realistic results, it has several limitations: Mainly, the live simulation is difficult to execute many times because of its cost and running time, so the design and the trial of command and control structures are difficult to iterate for many samples. Alternatively, researchers of command and control rely on constructive models to virtually regenerate the situation by representing commanders and units as computer models (Pew and Mavor 1998). Due to the nature of *agency* of commanders and units, the agent-based modeling and simulation (Bonabeau 2002) is one of the most frequent approaches to model. The agent-based models depict the individual process of perceiving the situation, deciding their own choices, and acting on the situation. For example, Soar (Laird et al. 1987) is a modeling framework to simulate an agent's cognitive and decision-making processes. Then, Plural Soar (Carley et al. 1992) is a model to simulate a collection of agents, and this model has been used to simulate the command and control of the air operation of the Army and the Air Force.

When multiple agents interact with others, the structure of the interaction is the command and control structure that the social network analysis is applied. Subsequently, there has been a research on merging the modeling and simulation with the social network. One of the notable works on merging the two approaches for the command and control research is a line of work conducted by Carley. Dynamic network analysis (Carley et al. 2007)—which is the overlapping area of modeling and simulation, social network analysis, and text analysis[2]—has been used to analyze the structure and the procedure of the command and control. The units and the commanders involved in command and control were represented as nodes and links of a social network. This social network is expanded further to include equipment, resources, pieces of information, diverse expertise, and assigned tasks as nodes; their associations and assignments are represented as links. This expanded social network resulted in a multimodal and multiplex network, so the expanded network is named the meta-network (Carley et al. 2002). By utilizing this meta-network concept, the organizational structure of the command and control is analyzed in a more informed way compared to using only agent interactions. Next to the network analyses on the meta-network, the agents on the meta-network are being modeled as agents in a multi-agent simulation. This agent-based modeling and simulation grants the dynamic nature to the network analysis. Originally, the social network analysis depended on a snapshot of a network that was taken at a certain point in the command and control procedure. However, by simulating the situation, we can see the dynamic changes of nodes and links that depict the changing command and control structure at multiple time

---

[2] Text analysis in the dynamic network analysis is used to capture the key elements in an organization from texts. For instance, a situation report can be analyzed by the text analysis to reproduce the organizational structure depicted on the report. Because this book is focused on modeling and simulating the structure, this identification stage of the command and control will not be introduced.

points. Further, the agents inherit the cognition, decision making, and the inter-action behavior of the previous agent models, such as Soar agents. Thus, the agents in the dynamic network analysis go beyond a simple node on a network; they are cognitive and interacting agents in command and control. This merging of modeling and simulation, the social network analysis, and the text analysis has been introduced in many ICCRTS proceedings. For example, the meta-network was introduced as a PCANS model in the 1998 ICCRTS (Krackhardt and Carley 1998).

1.3 Modeling Command and Control Under Extreme Situations

This book presents three case studies on how to model and simulate command and control in facing three different extreme situations. Each case study includes the result of analyzing organizational efficiency and mission accomplishment through modeling and simulation. Mainly, the agent-based modeling and simulation is used to capture the characteristics of commanders and units in the presented cases. As our first case study, we describe a model of a global terrorist network performing complex tasks (Moon and Carley 2007). Second, we model and simulate a naval air defense scenario that requires quick and accurate decision making (Kim et al. 2012). Finally, we describe the model of disaster response organizations facing a hurricane strike (Lee et al. 2012).

1.3.1 Modeling and Simulating Command and Control for Terrorist Organization

Over time, people change with whom they interact and where they are. For instance, terrorists attempt different tasks, move to new locations, and interact with different groups. Understanding how changes in social and geospatial relations interact is critical to a number of areas, including counterterrorism, counternar-cotics, and general social change. This case study introduces a simple theoretical multi-agent model for reasoning about the influence on the criticality of agents and locations as the distribution of agents in geospatial and the social interaction space coevolve. The model simulates social changes regarding with whom they interact and spatial changes in where they relocate as functions of learning and evolutions. The analysis suggests that terrorists will disperse around the world rather than gather at a specific location. Similarly, terrorists who have been at the center of social networks will be same. This model helps us gain insights into the com-plexities and social organizations evolving in social and geospatial dimensions simultaneously.

1.3.2 Modeling and Simulating Command and Control for Naval Air Defense

As the complexity of military operations increases, the defense modeling and simulation (DM&S) has contributed in analytically improving doctrines at the engineering, engagement, mission, and campaign levels. To date, defense modelers concentrate on the best representation of their targeted system at their targeted modeling level, and the modelers have parameterized and abstractly represented features that are not the prime concerns of their modeling level. However, insights from the battle experiment using such models are limited by the represented world of the model; the modelers are missing potential insights that might be gained if the modelers included more features in the simulation. Hence, to gain missed insights, this case study illustrates a battle experiment framework via the simulation interoperation of the heterogeneous levels of models. Our application is developing a mission-level doctrine for naval air defense scenarios, but a mission-level model alone does not represent the whole picture of the scenarios, and the model represents only the command and control procedures in detail, not the mechanical and engagement-level features. On the other hand, an engagement-level model depicts some of the missing parts of the scenarios in the mission-level model. Our finding is that we can gain new insights from performing battle experiments by interoperating two such models at the mission and engagement levels. Through the interoperation, input values of the mission-level model are generated from the engagement-level model dynamically, whereas the values were predefined parameters without the interoperation in the past. This dynamic value feed enables capture of the missing parts of the modeled scenarios at the mission level, eventually leading us to new insights. To demonstrate this improvement, this case study illustrates the different findings between the single model runs with predefined parameters and the interoperation model with dynamically generated parameters. We expect that this work will provide a new methodology for battle experiments by extending the limitation of single model representation of the real world.

1.3.3 Modeling and Simulating Command and Control for Disaster Response

Crisis management is critical in large-scale disaster situations. In a disaster situation, crisis management includes various operations, such as relaying relief resources to demanding places and organizations, providing basic support to evacuees, and starting recovery operations. These operations are not the purview of a single government organization but fall under the category of interorganizational cooperation. In spite of the importance of this cooperation, recent disasters (the Japanese tsunami, Hurricane Katrina) revealed inefficient and unorganized

organizational dynamics. Hence, this case study models and simulates the intra-
and interorganizational dynamics of relief organizations in Hurricane Katrina.
Particularly, we evaluate the model behavior from the network-centric operational
perspective, which is a prevalent concept for developing agile organizations in
crisis situations. Through the simulation, the network-centric operation measures
clearly describe the limitations in interorganizational cooperation; for instance, the
tardy resource delay even with the increasing number of cooperation links among
organizations, the limited shared situation awareness, and the failure to synchro-
nize action.

References

Alberts, D.S., Hayes, R.E.: Understanding command and control. Washington D.C.: U.S.
    Department of defense, command and control research program (2006)
Alberts, D.S., Nissen, M.E.: Toward harmonizing command and control with organization and
    management theory. Int. C2 J. **3**(2), 1–59 (2009)
Barton, A.H.: Social Organization Under Stress; A Sociological Review of Disaster Studies.
    National Academy of Sciences-National Research Council, Washington D.C (1963)
Bass, B.M.: Leadership: Good, better, best. Organ. Dyn. **13**(3), 26–40 (1985)
Berkowitz, B.D.: Information Age Intelligence. Foreign Policy **103**(Summer), 35–50 (1996)
Bittner, E.: The concept of organization. Soc. Res. **32**(3), 239–255 (1965)
Blanchard, B.S., Fabrycky, W.J.: Systems Engineering and Analysis, 5th edn. Prentice Hall, New
    York (2010)
Bonabeau, E.: Agent-based modeling: methods and techniques for simulating human systems.
    Proceedings of National Academy of Sciences. vol. 99, no. 3, pp. 7280–7287 (2002)
Brehmer, B.: The dynamic OODA loop: amalgamating boyd's OODA loop and the cybernetic
    approach to command and control. In: 10th international command and control research and
    technology symposium 2005
Brown, R.H.: Bureaucracy as praxis: toward a political phenomenology of formal organizations.
    Adm. Sci. Q. **23**(3), 365–382 (1978)
Builder, C.H., Banks, S.C., Nordin, R.: Command Concepts: A Theory Derived From The
    Practice of Command and Control. RAND, Washington (1999)
Carley, K.M., Newell, A.: The nature of the social agent. J. Math. Sociol. **19**(4), 221–262 (1994)
Carley, K.M., Kjaer-Hansen, J., Newell, A., Prietula, M.: Plural-Soar: A Prolegomenon to
    Artificial Agents and Organizational Behavior, in Artificial Intelligence in Organization and
    Management Theory, pp. 87–118. North-Holland, Amsterdam (1992)
Carley, K.M., Lee, J.S., Krackhardt, D.: Destabilizing networks. Connections **24**(3), 79–92
    (2002)
Carley, K.M., Diesner, J., Reminga, J., Tsvetovat, M.: Toward an interoperable dynamic network
    analysis toolkit. Decis. Support Syst. **43**(4), 1324–1347 (2007)
Comfort, L.K.: Crisis management in hindsight: cognition, communication, coordination, and
    control. Public Adm. Rev. **67**(1), 189–197 (2007)
Daly, J.J., Tolk, A.: Modeling and simulation integration with network-centric command and
    control architectures. In: Fall Simulation Interoperability Workshop 2003
Dynes, R.R., Tierney, K.J.: Disasters, Collective Behavior, and Social Organization. University
    of Delaware Press, Newark (1994)
Eisenhardt, K.M.: Agency theory: an assessment and review. Acad Manage. Rev. **14**(1), 67–74
    (1989)

Franklin, G.F., Powell, J.D., Emami-Naeini, A.: Feedback Control of Dynamic Systems, 6th edn. Prentice Hall, 2009

French, H.T., Hutchinson, A.: Measurement of situation awareness In a C4ISR experiment," In: 7th International Command and Control Research Technology Symposium (2002)

Friedkin, N.E.: Theoretical foundations for centrality measures. Am. J. Sociol. 96(6), 1478–1504 (1991)

Gold, A.H., Malhorta, A., Segars, A.: Knowledge Management: An Organizational Capabilities Perspective. J. Manage. Inf. Syst. 18(1), 185–214 (2001)

Guetzkowm, H., Simon, H.A.: The impact of certain communication nets upon organization and performance in task-oriented groups. Manage. Sci. 1(3), 233–250 (1955)

Harrald, J.R.: Agility and discipline: critical success factors for disaster response. ANN. Am. Acad. Polit. Soc. Sci. 604(1), 256–272 (2006)

Karasakal, O.: Air defense missile-target allocation models for a naval task group. Comput. Oper. Res. 35(6), 1759–1770 (2008)

Kim, J., Kim, T.G., Moon, I.C.: New insight into doctrine via simulation interoperation of heterogeneous levels of models in battle experimentation, simulation: transactions of the society for modeling and simulation. International 88(6), 649–667 (2012)

Krackhardt, D., Carley, K.M.: A PCANS model of structure in organizations. In: International Symposium on Command and Control Research and Technology 113–119 (1998)

Laird, J.E., Newell, A., Rosenbloom, P.S.: SOAR: An architecture for general intelligence. Artif. Intell. 33(1), 1–64 (1987)

Lee, G., Oh, N., Moon, I.C.: Modeling and Simulating Network-Centric Operations of Organizations for Crisis Management, in Spring Simulation Multiconference (2012)

Levchuk, Y.N., Pattipati, K., Curry, M.L., Shakeri, M.: Design of congruent organizational structures: Theory and algorithms, In:The 1996 Command and Control Research and Technology Symposium, 1996

Macal, C.M., North, M.J.: Tutorial on agent-based modelling and simulation. J. Simul. 4, 151–162 (2010)

March, J., Simon, H.A.: Organizations. Wiley, New York (1958)

McEntire, D.A.: Disaster response and recovery, 1st edn. Wiley, (2006)

McGuire, M.: Collaborative public management: assessing what we know and how we know it. Public Adm. Rev. 66(1), 33–43 (2006)

Mohr, L.B.: The concept of organizational goal. Am. Polit. Sci. Rev. 67(2), 470–481 (1973)

Moon, I.C., Carley, K.M.: Modeling and simulation of terrorist networks in social and geospatial dimensions. IEEE Intell. Syst. 22, 40–49 (2007)

Moon, I.-C.: Destabilization of adversarial organizations with strategic interventions, Carnegie Mellon University (2008)

Newman, M.E.J.: Clustering and preferential attachment in growing networks, Phys Rev E, vol. 64, no. 2, (2001)

Oliver, C.: Sustainable competitive advantage: combining institutional and resource-based views. Strateg. Manag. J. 18(9), 697–713 (1997)

Perrow, C.: Complex Organizations. Random House, New York (1986)

Peters, B.G., Pierre, J.: Governance without government? rethinking public administration. J. Public Adm. Res. Theory 8(2), 223–243 (1998)

Pew, R.W., Mavor, A.S.: Modeling Human and Organizational Behavior: Application to Military Simulations. National Academies Press, Washington D.C (1998)

Rosen, J., Grigg, E., Lanier, J., McGrath, S., Lillibridge, S., Sargent, D., Koop, C.E.: The future of command and control for disaster response. IEEE Eng. Med. Biol. Mag. 21(5), 56–68 (2002)

Wasserman, S. Faust, K.: Social Network Analysis: Methods and Applications, 1st edn. Cambridge University Press, Cambridge (1994)

Sageman, M.: Understanding Terror Networks. University of Pennsylvania Press, Philadelpia (2004)

Simon, H.A.: On the concept of organizational goal. Adm. Sci. Q. 9(1), 1–22 (1964)

Sorokin, P.A.: Man and Society in Calamity; The Effects of War, Revolution, Famine, Pestilence Upon Human Mind, Behavior, Social Organization and Cultural Life. E. P. Dutton & Co, New York (1942)

Stadler, N., Ben-Ari, E., Mesterman, E.: Terror, Aid and Organization: The Haredi Disaster Victim Identification Teams (ZAKA) in Israel. Anthropol. Q. **78**(3), 619–651 (2005)

Suh, N.P.: Complexity: Theory and Applications. Oxford University Press, New York (2005)

Tolk, A.: Engineering Principles of Combat Modeling and Distributed Simulation, 1st edn. John Wiley & Sons, Inc., Hoboken, New Jersey (2012)

U.S. Department of Defense, The Command and Control Research Program. http://www.dodccrp.org/. (2013). Accessed 01 Jan 2013

U.S. Joint Chiefs of Staff, Department of Defense Dictionary opf Military and Associated Terms. Washington D.C., p. 74, (1986)

Weber, M.: Theory of Social and Economic Organization. Oxford University Press, New York (1947)

White, H., Boorman, S., Breiger, R.: Social structure from multiple networks: blockmodels of roles and positions. Am. J. Sociol. **81**, 730–780 (1976)

Yuchtman, E., Seashore, S.E.: A system resource approach to organizational effectiveness. Am. Sociol. Rev. **32**(6), 891–903 (1967)

Yuki, G.A., Van Fleet, D.D.: Cross-situational, multimethod research on military leader effectiveness. Organ. Behav. Hum. Perform. **30**(1), 87–108 (1982)

Chapter 2
Modeling and Simulating Command and Control for Terrorist Organization

Keywords Command and control · Organizational goal · Geospace · Global terrorist network · Transactive memory · Dynet · OrgaHead · Construct · Meta-network · AutoMap · Multiagent simulation · Homophily · Knowledge diffusion · Task accuracy · Sensitivity analysis · Gini coefficient · Meta model

2.1 Introduction

As the command and control is an effort to achieve the organizational goal, the command and control structure should be designed to optimize crucial factors affecting the outcome. The interaction structure between the commanders and the units is one of such factors, and their geospatial locations are another critical factor. This is particularly significant when we consider a command and control structure that spans social groups as well as covers large geospace, i.e., a global terrorist network. We analyze the command and control structure of a global terrorist network[1] that we estimate from network text analyses.

Fundamentally, where social agents are influences who the agents know, and vice versa. As the agents move to new cities or countries, their contacts change. For instance, when a company relocates employees, they develop new working relations with others while they perform assigned tasks. In theory, relocation should improve performance. However, we also know that performance is dependent on knowing who to ask about what, i.e., transactive memory (Wegner 1986). Moving disrupts this memory and also the social relations by which information flows. Thus, we ask whether performance can improve when the geospatial and social distribution change simultaneously.

---

[1] This case study is introduced by Moon and Carley (2007). This chapter expands the initial publication with additional background, dataset description, and virtual experiment results. Also, at the end of this chapter, we discuss how to interpret the result in the context of the command and control.

I.-C. Moon et al., *Modeling and Simulating Command and Control*, SpringerBriefs in Computer Science, DOI: 10.1007/978-1-4471-5037-4_2, © Il-Chul Moon 2013

These social and spatial relations evolve over time, so does the command and control structure that the relations imply. Estimating the evolutions is an important issue for management, command and control structure, and intelligence analysis research. By knowing the future social and spatial distributions of agents, an analyst can identify who will be an emergent leader, where will be a hot spot, and what will be the vulnerability of the organization.

Historically, the estimation has heavily depended on qualitative analysis (Arquilla and Ronfeldt 2001) by subject matter experts. A few researchers have approached this issue using multi-agent models and simulation from two perspectives, the impact of change in the social network (Carley et al. 2001; Snijder et al. forthcoming) and the impact of geospatial change (Epstein et al. 2001; Bergkvist et al. 2004). Their models consider the complex nature of the organization and task assignments, resource distributions or the location of the agents. These models were used to simulate the near-term changes of the organizations. Both models are able to project the aspects of future performance and the emerging structure of an organization, but they cannot examine the interaction between physical and social movements.

In this chapter, we develop a simple theoretical multi-agent model that includes the social and the geospatial dimensions at the same time. We expand an existing social simulation model, Dynet (Carley 2003). The agents in the model interact with others as well as relocate themselves to other spatial locations. This model illustrates some of the ways in which group behavior can be affected by the coevolution of social and geospatial relations. Using this model, a theoretical study of the interaction between social and geospatial change is conducted. The focus here is on how changes in the social and geospatial relations, e.g., through the attrition or movement of critical actors defined using social network techniques, influences group behavior. Then, we ground the final results by examining the implications of the model for a real-world organization, a terrorist network. This latter examination is meant to illustrate the potential for reasoning with this type of model. While the results are informative, we note that additional work needs to be done in the field prior to a full validation study, particularly given the weakness of the extant data sets. The data we use are extracted using a network text analysis technique on open source texts.

2.2 Previous Research

The study of the concurrent movement of people through social relations and space has been done mainly using two techniques: data mining and simulation. Data mining has been used to detect the patterns from a large database, and the patterns include the organizational structure network, the entity properties, the clusters of entities, etc. For instance, Jonas and Harper summarized the impact of data mining on the counterterrorism community (Jonas and Harper 2006). First, they claim that the 9/11 attack plan was available to the U.S. Government prior to the attack. The plan could be obtained from an extensive data mining on available databases, and the government might have disrupted the plan if they pursue the available leads. Whereas they introduced the importance of data mining in the field, they also suggest that the high false positive, or incorrect prediction, may waste valuable resources.

Link analysis and discovery is also another data-mining technique used to address counterterrorism. Mooney et al. present a method, inductive logic programming, which can discover implied rules in the multi-relational data (Mooney et al. 2004). When an analyst has an incomplete organizational network, this method will be a powerful tool to approximate the complete network.

On the contrary, modeling and simulation have also been used to analyze real-world problems. For instance, Janeja et al. presented a work focusing on the detection of anomalous geospatial trajectories based on spatio-semantic associations (Janeja et al. 2004). This spatio-semantic association is similar to our correlation between the spatial and the social dimensions. In their chapter, they create basic spatial analysis units, or spatial units. Then, the spatial units are clustered and consist of a micro neighborhood that shares similar characteristics across the sub spatial units. This analysis is interesting because they regard the spatial and the social aspects at the same time.

As another example of computing with social and geospatial issues, Chen et al. wrote a chapter describing the development of the informatics and intelligence model (Chen et al. 2004). They examine three interesting usages, cross-jurisdiction information sharing; terrorism information collection; as well as smart border and bioterrorism application; based on the intelligence and security informatics approach. Their approaches heavily depend on the network and link analysis. Furthermore, one of their models, West Nile Virus-Botulism Portal, has hot spot analysis and prediction function.

Organizational behavior research has benefited from using agent-based modeling techniques. For instance, Carley shows the efforts to model the socio-technical systems as networked multi-agent structures (Carley 2002). She introduces exemplary multi-agent models, such as OrgaHead (Carley and Svoboda 1996) and Construct (Schreiber and Carley 2004). These models take network organizational structure as an input and generate the estimated performance over time as well as the evolved network structures after the simulation. This approach may be difficult to validate, or some may argue that it does not reflect all of the real-world aspects, so the estimation may be misguiding. Meanwhile, this is an effort to create more complex and realistic models that can automatically generate hypotheses forecasting the organizational behavior (Carley 1999). Then, these hypotheses can estimate what the features or trends of interest in the domain, which will lead the validation of hypotheses by other statistical analysis tools, such as data mining.

2.3 Organizational Structure of Terrorist Network

The introduction of this book explains the necessity to expand the simple network or the tree structure between commanders and units to represent the full elements of the command and control. One of the expanded representations is the meta-network. This section explains the meta-network and shows how to apply the meta-network representation to data of organizational elements.

2.3.1 Meta-Network for Organizational Structure

A meta-network (Krackhardt and Carley 1998; Carley 2002) is a multi-mode and multi-relation network that this case study utilizes to represent an organizational structure. We might describe it using a matrix of relations as in Table 2.1. From an organizational task perspective, there are four basic types of nodes of interest: people, knowledge, resources, and tasks, and other extensive types of nodes, i.e., location, belief, event, organization, etc., can be included. The relations among these who interacted with whom, who has access to what resources, what has what knowledge or expertise, who can or has done what task, what resources are needed for what task, and what knowledge is needed for what task or to use what resource. Each of these can be observed, with some level of uncertainty, and for many groups only in an "after the fact" fashion. In Table 2.1, for the sake of illustration, we define a possible network for each of the cells.

Meta-network is not just limited to a social network, which is only one part of meta-network. Meta-network covers much broader concepts related to organizational structure. These concepts are task assignment, resource distribution, information diffusion, resource requirements for tasks, and so on. Since this is not just social relationship information, analysts can store any of their knowledge regarding how the adversarial organizations structured for, prepared for, and executed the tasks. For instance, Task Precedence Network in Table 2.1 is more commonly analyzed by analysts in the operations research field. Information

Table 2.1 Meta-network component networks

	People	Knowledge	Resources	Tasks
People	Social network	Knowledge network	Resource network	Assignment network
Knowledge		Information network	Skills network	Knowledge needs network
Resources			Substitution network	Resource needs network
Tasks				Task precedence network

Network in Table 2.1 is a frequent topic for the information scientists researching knowledge management system or knowledge map. However, all of these concepts are critical factors in understanding how an organization operates, and these concepts can be systematically stored in a meta-network. This additional information of the organizations enable each component of this integrated analysis framework.

2.3.2 Estimated Terrorist Network in Meta-Network Format

An input to this model is a network representation of the organizational structure in the social and geospatial dimensions. Additionally, information on knowledge, tasks, and who knows and is doing what are used. Therefore, the input is a large network across a set of different nodes: agents, knowledge, tasks, and locations. For instance, if there have been interactions or formal relations between two agents, we assume that there is a link between the two. Similarly, if an agent possesses a knowledge piece, then we link the agent node to the knowledge node. If two locations appear in the same context, we regard the two locations are related. This topological location networks will be the agent relocation dimension. The other sub-networks have their own intuitive interpretations based on the connected node types. We use this multi-mode and multi-link network data as our input to the model with the assumption that it represents the current structural characteristics of the organization. Our model is applied to a terrorist network that extracted from open source or unclassified documents, such as newspapers and intelligence reports from subject matter experts using the AutoMap software (Diesner and Carley 2005), and then with supplemental hand coding to add latitude and longitude. Additional information on the coding process is provided by Carley

Table 2.2 Meta-network of the organizational structure for this case study

	Agent	Knowledge	Task	Location
Agent (916 agents, A)	Social network (AA, 0.0024)	Knowledge network (AK, 0.0093)	Assignment network (AT, 0.0070)	Deploy network (AL, 0.0026)
Knowledge (614 knowledge bits, K)		Not used	Needs network (KT, 0.0961)	Regional knowledge network (KL, 0.0692)
Task (258 tasks, T)			Not used	Regional task network (TL, 0.1042)
Location (387 locations, L)				Proximity network (LL, 0.0799)

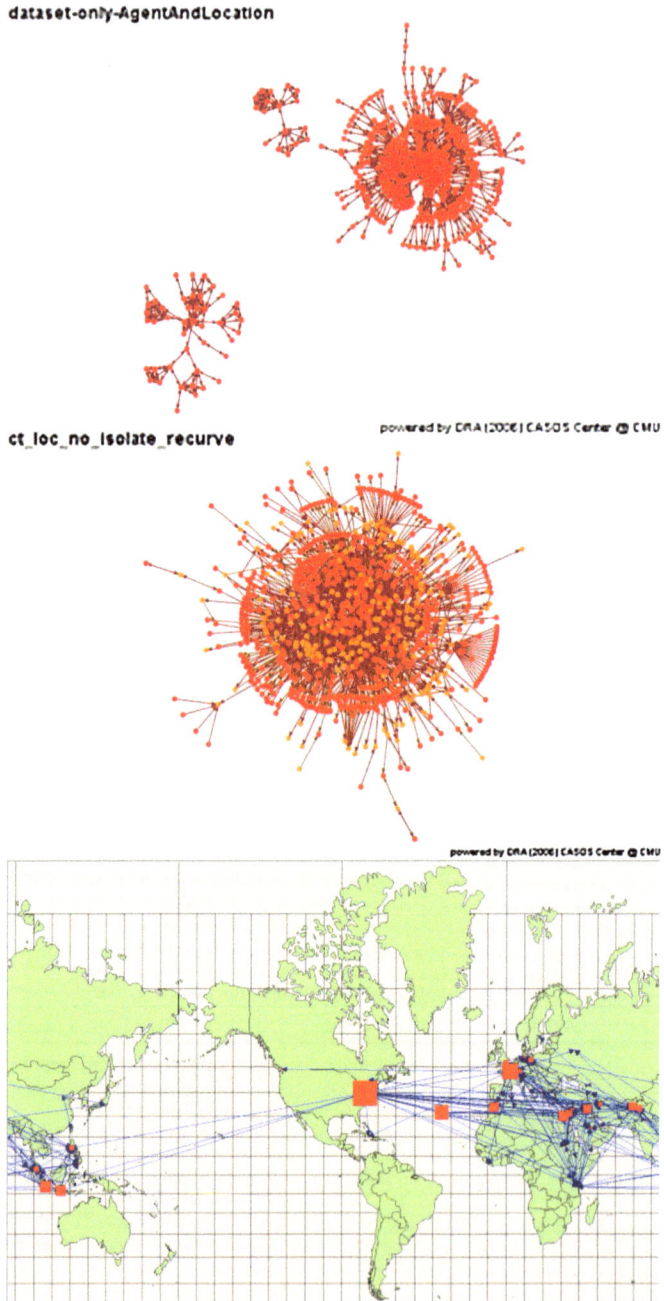

Fig. 2.1 (*Top*) Social network between agents, or AA in Table 2.2, (*Middle*) deploy network of agents, or AL in Table 2.2, (*Bottom*) World map of agent deployments and social interactions between deployed agents

et al. (forthcoming). After the network-text analyses and the dataset cleaning, we display the meta-matrix of the input dataset with descriptive statistics in Table 2.2. The numbers in cells of Table 2.2 represent the network density. Also, Fig. 2.1 visualizes some of the networks in the Table 2.2.

2.4 Modeling Command and Control on Social and Geospatial Dimensions

We introduce a multi-agent simulation model that overcomes the limitations, such as isolated social and geospatial models. To model the social dimension, the agent interaction algorithm specifies the probability of interaction between two agents. Also, for the geospatial dimension, the agent relocation mechanism concerns the agent movement on the geospatial location network in a dataset. The initial social network and geospatial information are drawn from real data for a group. The model output reveals important aspects of the evolved complex organization.

2.4.1 Model Summary

To estimate changes overtime in the performance and structure of organization, the model simulates each individual agent and the agent's interaction with others. As agent interact and learn, their behavior will eventually change the organizational structure and performance. These mechanisms are outlined as a flowchart in Fig. 2.2. Basically, the agents can interact and relocate at each time step. Agents select a location to move and an agent to interact with. The selection is based on the probabilistic values for each interaction and relocation opportunities. Exactly which agent interacts with which, when, what choices they make, and what they communicate and learn are defined probabilistically. Consequently, the model is stochastic, and as such multiple replications are needed to generate stable results and to define the space of outcomes.

Additionally, as listed in Table 2.3, there are several factors, which drive the agent behavior and so the evolution of the network. The parameters concern the interaction radius on the social dimension, the relocation radius on the geospatial dimension, the probability of learning after a knowledge exchange with an agent, or a knowledge gathering at a certain location, etc. Agent behavior also depends on the given input dataset, as this sets their initial environment. The input determines the initial probability of interaction among agents as this is based on what knowledge they have and where they are located. This model has two levels of parameters. Finally, there are factors driving an agent's behavior, calculated from the used defined parameters, inputs, and various formulas.

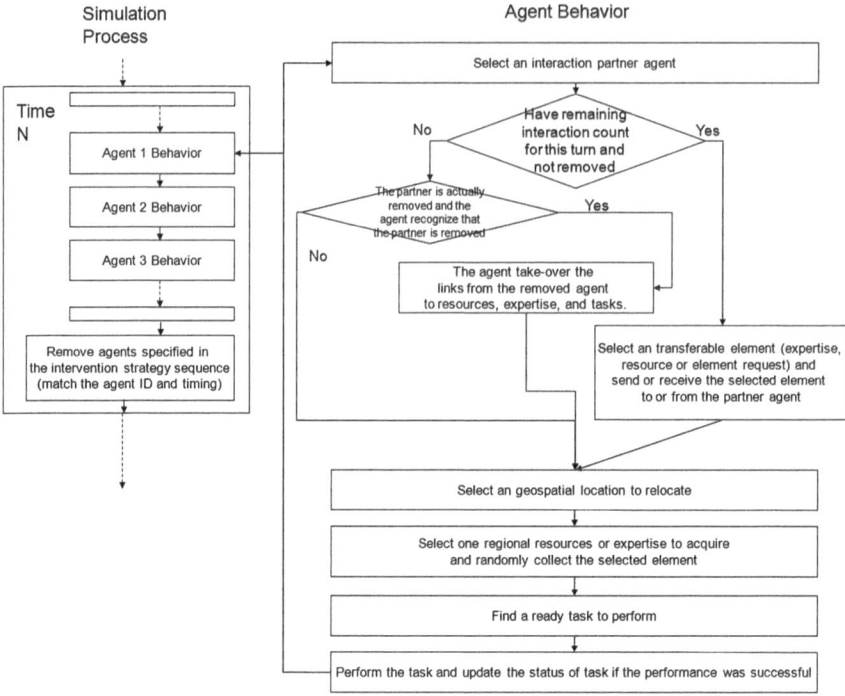

Fig. 2.2 Flowchart describing the simulation progress and the agent behavior

We test this model by varying some important parameters in the agent inter-actions and relocations. Table 2.4 is the design of such variations, and this pro-vides the sensitivity of the results when exact parameter values are impossible to obtain. First, we change the agent move radius by zero, one, and two. If an agent has zero move radius, then the agent is stationary to his initial location. On the contrary, two move radius means that the agents can search locations linked by two location-to-location links from their initial locations. Next, we vary the weight of relative similarity and expertise contributing to the probability interaction. If the weight of relative similarity is high, the agents mainly interact with agents sharing backgrounds, belief, and knowledge. This imitates that the agents are passive information receivers. In contrast, higher relative expertise weight makes the agents active information seekers. Third, we test the sensitivity of the input data by randomly dropping or adding links in the agent-to-agent network or location-to-location network.

To reason the effect of the parameter variations, we need to describe the details of the agent behavior in the social and the geospatial dimensions. The next section describes such agent behavior.

Table 2.3 List of input variables, output variables, parameters, and major model internal variables of the model

Type	Name	Implication
Input	A networked organizational structure	A network including agents, knowledge pieces, tasks, and locations. The network represents the complex organizational structure of the target domain.
Output	An evolved network organization	An evolved network organization with a recreated agent-to-agent network and a agent-to-location network based on interactions and relocations
	Knowledge diffusion	A performance metric showing how fast the information can be diffused across the network
	Energy task accuracy	A performance metric showing how accurately the information are distributed to the agents who require it for their task completion
	Gini coefficient for AA and AL	Gini coefficients indicating the extent of unequal distribution of criticalities of agent-to-agent network and agent-to-location network
Parameters	Simulation run time step (default: 30)	Total simulation run time
	Number of replication (default : 3)	Number of model runs, required since this is a stochastic model, not a deterministic model
	Move radius (MR)	The radius on the spatial route network specifying an agent's maximum move radius in one time step
	Vision range (VR) (default: 1)	The range on the spatial route network specifying an agent ability to gather a knowledge piece or interact with another agent
	Sphere of influence (SI) (default: 2)	The number of social links that an agent can cross for an interaction
	Weight for relative similarity (w_1), For relative expertise (w_2), for social distance (w_3) (default: 0.5), for spatial proximity (w_4) (default: 0.5)	Weight for relative similarity when calculating the probability of interaction, for relative expertise when calculating the probability of interaction, for social distance when calculating the probability of interaction, and for spatial proximity when calculating the probability of interaction, respectively
	Learning rate from an agent (default: 0.05)	The possibility that an agent can learn a piece of information from an interaction with another agent
	Learning rate from a location (default: 0.025)	The possibility that an agent can gather a piece of information by observing a knowledge node within vision range
Internal variables	Relative similarity (RS_{ij})	Likelihood of interactions caused by homophily, also can be viewed as passive information seeking
	Relative expertise (RE_{ij})	Likelihood of interactions caused by expertise, also can be viewed as active information seeking
	Social distance (SD_{ij})	Difficulties of interactions over multiple social links
	Spatial proximity (SP_{ij})	Difficulties of interactions from spatial distance
	Interaction candidate set (ICS_i)	A set of agents who agent i can interact with
	Probability of interaction ($P_{ij}^{\text{Interaction}}$)	Likelihood of agent i's interaction with agent j, weighted linear sum of relative similarity, relative expertise, social distance, and spatial proximity
	Probability of Relocation ($P_{il}^{\text{Relocation}}$)	Likelihood of agent i's moving to location l, determined by the number of available knowledge bits required to perform the agents' assigned tasks

Table 2.4 Virtual experiment design to observe the sensitivity of the simulation results and to explore the parameter space

Name	Value	Implication
Move radius (*MR*)	0, 1, or 2 (3 cases)	Parameter space exploration, examining the sensitivity of the result according to the agent movement perimeter
Weights For Relative Similarity (w_1)/Relative Expertise (w_2)	0/1, 0.25/0.75, 0.6/0.4, 0.75/0.25, 1/0 (5 cases)	Parameter space exploration, examining the agent interaction attitudes and its impact to the results, from passive information gathering to active information gathering
Density of the organizational structure network (density of *AA* and *LL*)	75, 100, 125 % (3 cases)	Sensitivity analysis, examining the sensitivity of results according to the density changes of the *AA* and *LL* networks corresponding to the social dimension and geospatial dimension
Total virtual experiment cells	45 cells, (3 × 5 × 3 cases)	

2.4.1.1 Agent Interaction Mechanism

The agents in the model have the opportunity to interact with others each time period. They select an agent to interact with based on the probability of interaction that is a weighted sum of four different factors, relative similarity, relative expertise, social distance, and spatial proximity, explained in the sub-sections. The theory for these factors comes from sociology, communication theory, and counter-terrorism analysis.

As this is a stochastic model, an agent will most of the time interact with those agents whom they have a higher probability of choosing; but, on occasions (as dictated by this probability) will end up with a less likely choice. Like humans, these simulated agents cannot always talk to those they want most. This stochastic model captures this behavior of human intention being distinct from human action and the rare unexpected interaction.

After choosing an agent to interact, the two agents will exchange knowledge pieces. For each exchanged knowledge piece, a number will be drawn from a uniform distribution ranging from 0 to 1. If the number is under the learning rate for that agent, the receiving agent will have a new link to the communicated knowledge piece in the agent-to-knowledge network (AK).

- Relative similarity (RS) and relative expertise (RE): RS is the ratio reflecting the similarity in knowledge of the choosing and chosen agents. This is based on the sociological principle of homophily (McPherson et al. 2001; Kandel 1978; Gavrieli and Scott 2005). Homophily means that a person is likely to interact with another person sharing similar education, beliefs, or race. This represents the phenomena that terrorists often interact with other terrorists sharing the same religion or nationality. (RE) is a ratio reflecting the amount of knowledge the chosen agent has that the chooser does not have. This is based on the transactive memory (Wegner 1986; Hollingshead 2000; Mieg 2001). This captures why a Middle-East terrorist interact with a South American drug Cartel to exchange weapon expertise or information about funding sources. From a glimpse, the two factors may look contradictory, but these are just two metrics capturing different aspects of knowledge acquisition attitudes of terrorists.

$$RS_{ij} = \frac{\sum_{k=0}^{|K|} AK_{ik}AK_{jk}}{\sum_{k=0}^{|K|} AK_{ik}}, \quad RE_{ij} = \frac{\sum_{k=0}^{|K|} AK_{jk}(1 - AK_{ik})}{\sum_{k=0}^{|K|} AK_{ik}} \tag{2.1}$$

- Social distance (SD): The social distance, as shown in Formula 2.2, between the two agents is another factor affecting the probability of interaction. If two agents have to cross many social links, then the probability of interaction should be low, and vice versa (Watts et al. 2002; Friedkin 1983; Akerlof 1997). First, we find the shortest path between the two agents, and then we define SD as one over the number of links in the path. If the SD is larger than the maximum, SI, chosen by the user, it is set to one over the maximum for social interaction perimeter modeling. Agents in the model recognize and distinguish the closeness of other agents in the perimeter of SI, but they cannot differentiate the closeness when the interacting agent is outside of the perimeter. In this case, the agents regard the interacting agents are just SI + 1 links away though the real SD may be different.

$$SD_{ij} = \frac{1}{|AA_{ij}|}$$

$$|AA_{ij}| = \begin{cases} \text{num. of links on the shortest path from } i \text{ to } j \\ \qquad\qquad\qquad\qquad (\text{\# of links} \leq SI) \\ SI + 1 (\text{\# of links} > SI) \end{cases} \tag{2.2}$$

- Spatial proximity (SP): The spatial proximity, as defined in Formula 2.3, also factors in calculating the probability of interaction. Intuitively, two persons who are at the same location are more likely to talk than are those at different locations (Sorenson and Stuart 2001; Butts 2002; Sageman 2004). Some may argue that the SP is not significantly correlated with the frequency of the interaction in the age of Internet. However, in the terrorism domain, in the same training camp and going the same mosque are critical indicators of interactions (Sageman 2004). The SP model is the inverse of spatial distance and is used as an indicator of the probability of being at the same location. As with social distance, if social proximity is greater than the maximum chosen by user, it is set to one over the maximum for computing convenience.

$$SP_{ij} = \frac{1}{(|LL_{l_1 l_2}| + 1) AL_{i l_1} AL_{j l_2}}$$

$$|LL_{l_1 l_2}| = \begin{cases} \text{num. of links on the shortest path from } l_1 \text{ to } l_2 \\ (\# \text{ of links} \leq VR) \\ VR + 1 (\# \text{ of links} > VR) \end{cases} \tag{2.3}$$

- Probability of Interaction: The agents select another agent to interact with based on the probability of interaction, as specified in Formula 2.4. The probability is a weighted sum of four different factors explained above. We standardize the factors by dividing them with the maximum value of the interaction candidate sets (defined below).

$$P_{ij}^{\text{Interaction}} = w_1 RS_{ij} + w_2 RE_{ij} + w_3 SD_{ij} + w_4 SP_{ij} \tag{2.4}$$

Though the probability can be calculated for any pair of two agents, we limit the number of possible interaction candidate agents. The candidate agents are chosen based on two distances, SD and spatial proximity. This is an assumption that a person will interact with others in their neighborhoods—either the social neighborhood or the geographic one. Formally, the candidate agent set is defined using Formula 2.5. An agent can communicate only with his candidate agents, so the probability of interaction is calculated between each agent and that agent's candidate agents.

$$ICS_i = \{A_j | (|AA_{ij}| \leq SI) \vee (|LL_{l_1 l_2}| AL_{i l_1} AL_{j l_2} \leq VR)\} \tag{2.5}$$

2.4.1.2 Agent Relocation Mechanism

The agents in the model are capable of relocating themselves to other adjacent locations. The sphere of relocation is determined by a parameter, move radius (MR), but the probability to choose a certain location is calculated by more complicated formula, Formula 2.6. In essence, the agents choose a location which on average guarantees the shortest path to their required knowledge pieces. In other words, the agents try to put themselves at the optimal location to collect the knowledge they want. However, just like the agent-to-agent interaction model, this is a stochastic model with the choice of location determined probabilistically. Hence, it is possible to choose a nonpreferable location with lower probability.

$$P_{il}^{\text{Reloaction}} = \cfrac{1}{\sum\limits_{t=0}^{|T|}\sum\limits_{k=0}^{|K|} \text{AT}_{it} \times \text{KT}_{kt} \times |\text{KL}_{kl}|}$$

$$|\text{KL}_{kl}| = \begin{cases} \text{num. of links on the shortest path from } l \text{ to } k \\ \qquad\qquad\qquad (\#\ \text{of links} \leq \text{VR}) \\ \qquad\qquad \text{VR} + 1(\#\ \text{of links} > \text{VR}) \end{cases} \qquad (2.6)$$

After selecting a location, the model changes the agent-to-location network (AL) by removing the edge from the agent to the old location and adding an edge from the agent to the new location. Additionally, the agent will gather knowledge pieces linked to locations within vision range (VR). This knowledge gathering is similar to the knowledge exchange between agents except using a different learning rate. Some may argue that this regional knowledge acquisition may not be true, especially in the real world where terrorists can learn new knowledge from web sites. However, it should be noted that many terrorists go training sites and headquarters of terrorist organizations to receive specific and detailed training. These terrorists' relocations are an important issue in the counterterrorism field (Sageman 2004), and we are specifically examining such relocations in this chapter.

2.4.1.3 Output Measures

To assess the change of the organization, we have two performance metrics. The performance metrics are used to evaluate the performance of the evolving organization over time. There are two performance metrics, knowledge diffusion and energy task accuracy. Knowledge diffusion (Formula 2.7) gauges the dispersion of the knowledge bits across the agents.

$$\text{KD} = \frac{\sum\limits_{i=0}^{|A|}\sum\limits_{j=0}^{|K|} \text{AK}_{ij}}{|K| \times |A|} \qquad (2.7)$$

Knowledge diffusion only considers who knows what. Whereas, energy task accuracy (Formula 2.8) calculates the extent to which the agents have the knowledge they need to do the tasks they are assigned. This is done by introducing the agent-to-task (AT) and knowledge-to-task (KT) network in the formula. In Formula 2.8, C indicates a constant term.

$$\text{ETA} = \frac{C}{|T|}\sum\limits_{t=0}^{|T|} \frac{\sum\limits_{k=0}^{|K|}\left(\text{KT}_{kt} \times \sum\limits_{a=0}^{|A|} \text{AK}_{ak}\right)}{\sum\limits_{a=0}^{|A|} \text{AT}_{at} \times \sum\limits_{k=0}^{|K|} \text{KT}_{kt}} \qquad (2.8)$$

Furthermore, we define two criticality metrics for the agents and locations. For agents, we count the number of agents that an agent had interacted with during the simulation. This represents the number of agents that the agents know and influenced. For locations, we count the number of agents in a location at the end time. If the location harbors more agents, the location may have higher terrorist activities.

2.5 Result

The terrorist network in the meta-matrix format is analyzed by the presented agent-based model, and the model generates estimates on the agent relocation, the geospatial clustering, the agent interaction, and the social network evolution. First, we perform a sensitivity analysis. Then, we visualize and analyze the model output in two dimensions.

2.5.1 Sensitivity Analysis

The sensitivity analysis of this model is performed by varying the important input parameters (refer Table 2.3). After running the model with varied parameters, we perform a regression analysis. The independent variables are the varied parameters of a virtual experiment cell. The dependent variables are the two performance metrics and the Gini coefficients of the agent and location criticality distributions.

Table 2.5 is the regression analysis result. First, as MR increases, the performance of the network gets better. This suggests that the terrorists are distributed where they are not receiving the best information from regions and they will relocate to find better places to obtain the information. Furthermore, these relocations will increase their task performance by increasing the information feed. Next, higher MR and higher possible density decreases the Gini coefficient of location criticalities. This illustrates that the terrorists will be dispersed more if they can relocate easier and the input network is denser. Finally, lower RS will induce a more centralized terrorist network. Particularly, the input network density impacts the agent criticality distribution greatly compared to the impact to the location criticality.

2.5.2 Analysis of Location Criticality

The agent movement creates segregation patterns over time, Fig. 2.3. For analysis, we draw an accumulated agent distribution across the locations, Fig. 2.4. The figure implies that the agents will be dispersed more if we increase the move radius. If there are few appropriate places where terrorists can harbor, the increased MR will allow more terrorists to find the places and to be clustered

Table 2.5 Meta-model regression analysis for sensitivity analysis

Dependent variable		Energy task accuracy	Knowledge diffusion	Gini coefficient of location criticality dist.	Gini coefficient of agent crtiicality dist.
Standardized coefficients	Move radius	0.748^*	0.780^*	-0.956^*	-0.088
	Relative similarity	0.008	0.004	0.020	0.131^+
	Possible density	0.010	0.009	-0.114^*	-0.865^*
Adjusted R^2		0.506	0.555	0.925	0.765

[+] P value < 0.01, *P value < 0.001

around the places. However, our model indicates the opposite scenario. The terrorists in our model are not able to find the places where they can cluster densely. Rather than gathering in few regions, the terrorists will disperse around the world.

Next, we list the top ten locations harboring terrorists after simulations, Table 2.6. While the accumulated distribution and its Gini coefficient, in Fig. 2.4, illustrate the terrorists will disperse, the listed top ten locations are pretty consistent across three different MR level. This implies that the hot regions with frequent terrorist activities will remain at the top after the relocations though some of the terrorist at the location will move to other non terrorism-intensive regions. In detail, the Northwest African regions, i.e., Morocco and Casablanca, get important as well as some European regions, France and Strasbourg. The south Asian regions, Indonesia and Bali, and the area with frequent activities, US, Iraq, and Israel, will hold status quo.

2.5.3 Analysis of Agent Criticality

We analyze the importance of agents after the simulation. According to the sensitivity analysis, the changes of RS impact the distribution of the agent criticality. Therefore, in Fig. 2.5, we visualize the accumulated agents' social link coverage across the levels of relative similarity. While we can see some slight difference in terms of Gini coefficients, the distribution of link coverage does not change much. This implies that the evolution of the terrorist social network is stable regardless of the parameter change. In spite of the small changes, the increasing Gini coefficient as the higher RS suggest that the social links will be controlled by fewer terrorists, if terrorists gather information more passively. For instance, a group of terrorists often have different backgrounds from another group of terrorists. In that case, under a strong RS interaction weight, only terrorists who have both backgrounds of the two groups will be able to communicate with the members from both groups. This means that there will be fewer agents likely to talk to under strong homophily trend, and these few agents will control more social links.

Like the location criticality analysis, we list the top ten terrorists who control most of links after simulation, Table 2.7. The table shows that the top terrorists, i.e.

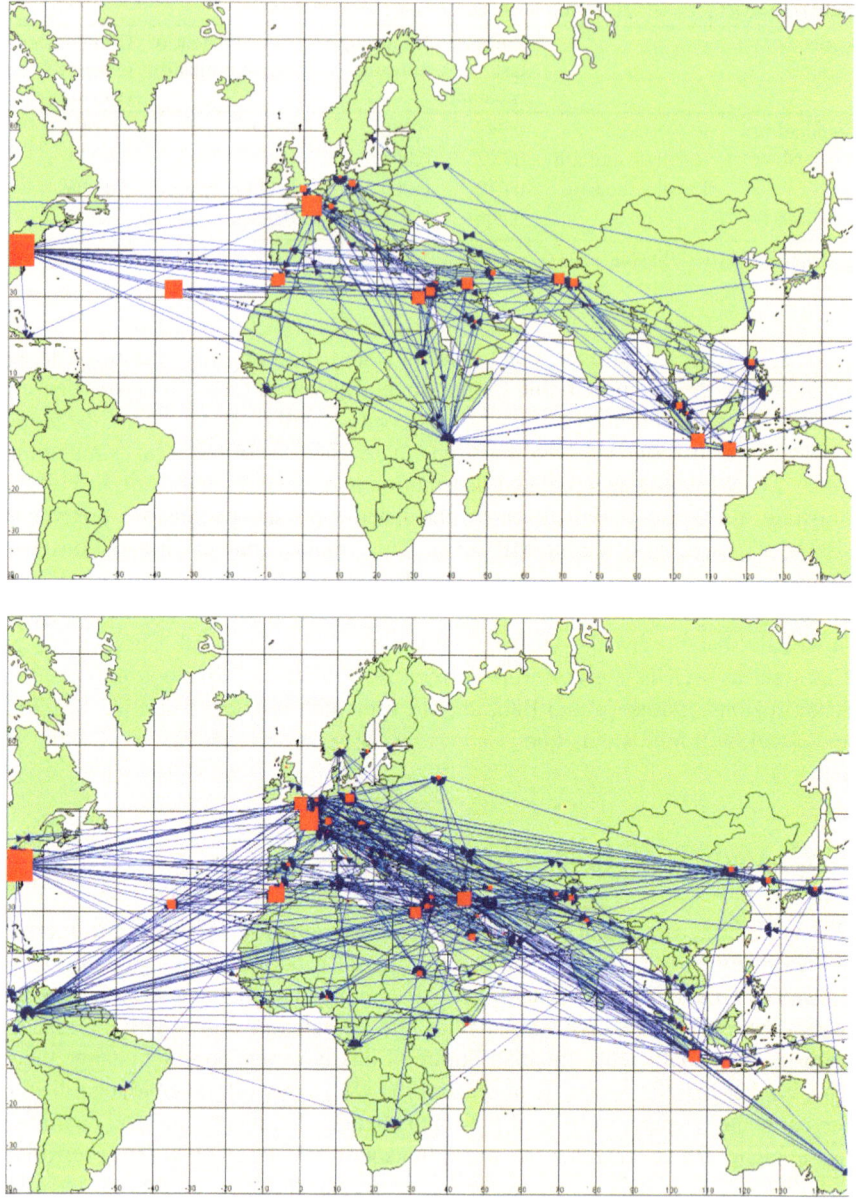

Fig. 2.3 (*Top*) the initial deployment of agents and their social interactions across regions (*Bottom*) the converged deployment of agents and their social interactions when the move radius is set to be one

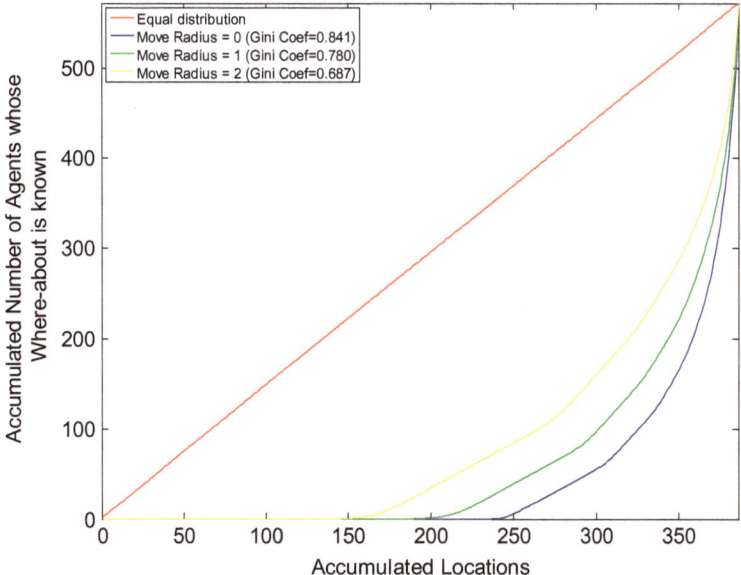

Fig. 2.4 Accumulated distribution of agents across the regions. 570 agents were deployed to 387 locations

Table 2.6 The top ten locations that the agents were deployed to

Rank	Move radius : 0 (Stationary case)	Move radius : 1 (adjacent move)	Move radius : 2 (farther move)
1	u_s	u_s	u_s
2	Israel	France	France
3	France	Morocco	Morocco
4	Bali	Israel	Casablanca
5	Morocco	Bali	Bali
6	Egypt	Casablanca	Egypt
7	Afghanistan	Egypt	Israel
8	Casablanca	Iraq	Strasbourg
9	Iraq	Indonesia	Gaza
10	Indonesia	Strasbourg	Indonesia

Bin Laden or Riduan Isamuddin, will have similar power after simulations in spite of varying parameters. This is because they are already in the center of the social networks among terrorists, so they appear in the interaction candidate sets frequently. Additionally, they have pretty comprehensive backgrounds and knowledge which most of the agents can find high RS and expertise at the same time. On the other hand, Mohammad Atta will have higher ranks under passive information gathering assumption, since his background is common across the agents.

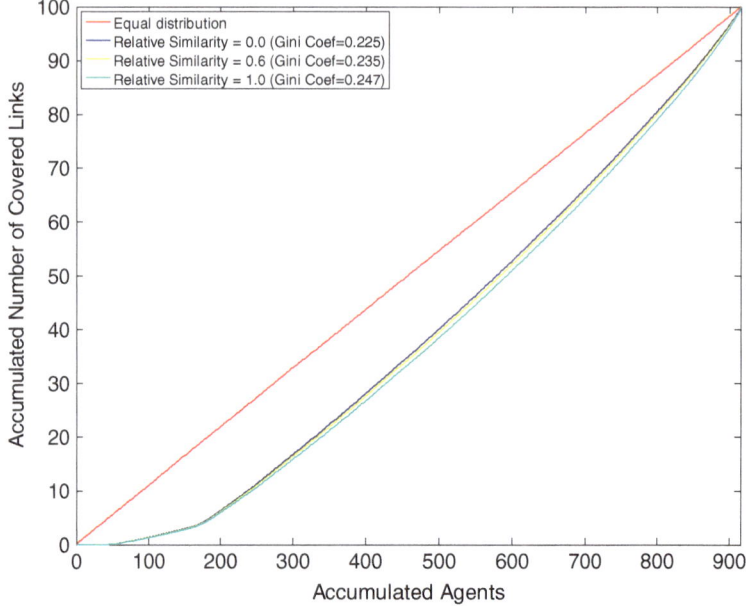

Fig. 2.5 Accumulated distribution of the percentage of covered social links by agents

Table 2.7 The top ten agents that have the highest number of social links to other agents

Rank	Relative similarity : 0.0 (active information gathering)	Relative similarity : 0.6	Relative similarity : 1.0 (passive information gathering)
1	bin_laden	bin_laden	bin_laden
2	riduan_isamuddin	riduan_isamuddin	riduan_isamuddin
3	abdul_aziz	abdul_aziz	mohammed_atta
4	yasser_arafat	yasser_arafat	bakar_bashir
5	bakar_bashir	yaacov_perry	yasser_arafat
6	mohammed_atta	mohammed_atta	zacarias_moussaoi
7	yaacov_perry	bakar_bashir	yaacov_perry
8	imam_samudra	zacarias_moussao	abdul_aziz
9	zacarias_moussao	mohambedou_slah	yazid_sufaat
10	abdullah_sungkar	abdullah_sungkar	mohambedou_slah

2.6 Lessons Learned to Model and Simulate Command and Control

This case study introduces a model and simulation results describing the location criticality and the agent criticality changes over time by using the command and control structure of terrorists discovered from network text analysis on open source documents. The model is a multi-agent simulation model, and we estimate the collective behavior of this networked organization based on our agent behavior mechanism. The agent behavior mechanism consists of two parts, social interaction and geospatial relocation. Based on the input networked organization and the agent behavior, we calculated and analyze the performance, the geospatial distribution, and the interaction log records during the simulation period.

The model and its simulation results indicate the evolution of command and control structure in two modeled dimensions: social and geospatial dimensions. Our analysis indicates that the agents will become more dispersed around the world in the geospatial dimension. In the perspective of location criticality, some regions, such as North America and Middle Eastern Asia, will hold their status quo. On the other hand, some locations, i.e., Europe and North Western Africa, may gain more agents. The critical agents do not change much in the social dimension. Some of the changes are expected according to the agents' information gathering model. If the terrorists gather information passively, Mohammad Atta or Bakar Bashir will gain more power. Meanwhile, well-known key terrorists like Bin Laden or Riduan Isamuddin will hold their powers regardless of agent interaction trend changes. This modeling and simulation result would have limitations in several aspects. First of all, the validity of the results with the given dataset is very limited. The simulation model takes in the limited facet of the real world, and the model would not reflect the reality with the given limitation. Further, the model is very illustrative and simple, so the model would not show the agent behavior with the fine details of the real world.

In spite of this limitation, this case study investigates how the command and control structures rest in multiple dimensions interact with. In the real world, the command and control structure is embedded in multiple spaces that differ in nature. If we redeploy units and commanders in the geospace, we have to readjust the command and control structure in the social space. Similarly, if units and commanders have different chain of commands, this may indicate the units and the commanders have changes in other spaces that are factors of the command and control. Though this case study models only two different spaces, as the modeled behavior of command and control gets complicated, the modelers of command and control should add more dimensions of interests to the simulation model.

References

Akerlof, G.A.: Social distance and social decisions. Econometrica. **65**(5), 1005–1027 (1997)

Arquilla, J., D. Ronfeldt (eds.).: Networks and netwars: the future of terror, crime, and militancy. Santa Monica, Calif: RAND, MR-1382-OSD. www.rand.org/publica-tions/MR/MR1382/ (2001)

Bergkvist, M., Davidson, P., Persson, J.A., Ramstedt, L.: A hybrid micro-simulator for determining the effects of governmental control policies on transport chains. Joint Work-shop on Multi-Agent and Multi-Agent Based Simulation. Springer, New York (2004)

Butts, C.T.: Spatial models of large-scale interpersonal networks. Doctoral Dissertation, Carnegie Mellon University (2002)

Carley, K.M., Lee, J.S., Krackhardt, D.: Destabilizing networks. Connections **24**(3), 31–44 (2001)

Carley, K.M.: Dynamic network analysis. Committee on Human Factors, National Research Council. pp. 133–145 (2003)

Carley, K.M.: Computational organization science: a new frontier.In: Proceedings of the National Academy of Science, vol. 99(3), pp. 7314–7316 (2002)

Carley, K.M., Svoboda, D.M.: Modeling organizational adaptation as a simulated annealing process. Sociol. Methods Res. **25**(1), 138–168 (1996)

Carley, K.M.: On generating hypotheses using computer simulations. Syst. Eng. **2**(2), 69–77 (1999)

Carley, K.M., Diesner, J., Reminga, J., Tsvetovat, M.: Toward an interoperable dynamic network analysis toolkit, DSS special issue on cyber infrastructure for homeland security: advances in information sharing, data mining, and collaboration systems, forthcoming

Carley, K.M.: Smart agents and organizations of the future, the handbook of new media. In: Lievrouw, L., Livingstone, S (eds.). Thousand Oaks, CA, Sage, Ch. 12, 206–220 (2002)

Chen, H., Wang, F., Zeng, D.: Intelligence and security informatics for homeland security: information, communication, and transportation. IEEE Trans. Intell. Transp. Syst. **5**(4), 329–341 (2004)

Diesner, J., Carley, K.M.: Revealing and comparing the organizational structure of covert networks with network text analysis. XXV Sunbelt Social Network Conference, Redondo Beach, 16–20 Feb (2005)

Epstein, J., Steinbruner, J.D., Parker, M.T.: Modeling Civil Violence: An Agent-Based Computational Approach. Center of Social and Economic Dynamics, Brookings Institute, Washington, D.C (2001)

Friedkin, N.E.: Horizons of observability and limits of informal control in organizations. Soc. Forces **62**, 54–77 (1983)

Gavrieli, D.A., Scott, W.R.: Intercultural knowledge flows in edge organizations: trust as an enabler. In: Proceeding of International Command and Control Research and Technology Symposium (2005)

Hollingshead, A.B.: Perceptions of Expertise and Transactive Memory in Work Relationships. Group Processes Intergroup Relat. **3**(3), 257–267 (2000)

Janeja, V.P., Atluri, V., Adam, N.R.: Detecting anomalous geospatial trajectories through spatial characterization and spatio-semantic associations.In: Proceedings of the 2004 Annual National Conference on Digital Government Research, pp. 1–10 (2004)

Jonas, J., Harper, J.: Effective Counterterrorism and the Limited Role of Predictive Data Minig, Policy Analysis, No. 584. CATO Institute, Dec 2006

Kandel, D.B.: Homophily, selection, and socialization in adolescent friendships, Am. J. Sociol. **84**(2), 427–436, 1978

Keller-McNulty, S., Bellman, K.L., Carley, K.M., Davis, P.K., Ivanetich, R., Laskey, K.B.: Defense Modeling, Simulation, and Analysis: Meeting the Challenge, The National Academies Press, pp. 64–73, (2006)

Krackhardt, D., Carley, K.M.: A PCANS model of structure in organization. In: Proceedings of the 1998 International Symposium ·on Command and Control Research and Technology, pp. 113–119, 1998e Challenge, The National Academies Press, pp. 64–73 (2006)

McPherson, M., Smith-Lovin, L., Cook, J.M.: Birds of a Feather: Homophily in Social Networks, Annual Review of Sociology, vol. 27, pp. 415–444 (2001)

Mieg, A.: The Social Psychology of Expertise: Case Studies in Research, Professional Domains, and Expert Roles. Erlbaum, Mahwah (2001)

Mooney, R.J., Melville, O., Tang, L.R., Shavlik, J., Dutra, I., Page, D., Costa, V.S.: Relational data mining with inductive logic programming for link discovery, in data mining: next generation challenges and future directions. In: Kargupta, H., Joshi, A., Siva-kumar K., and Yesha, Y. (eds.) pp. 239–254, AAAI Press, Menlo Park (2004)

Moon, I.C., Carley K.M.: Modeling and simulation of terrorist networks in social and geospatial dimensions. IEEE Intell. Sys. Special Issue on Social Computing **22**, 40–49, Sep/Oct (2007)

Reminga, J., Carley, K.M.: ORA: Organization Risk Analyzer, Tech Report, CMU-ISRI-04-106, CASOS. Carnegie Mellon University, Pittsburgh. http://www.casos.cs.cmu.edu/projects/ora/index.html(2004)

Sageman, M.: Understanding terror networks. University of Pennsylvania Press, Philadelphia, pp. 142–146 (2004)

Schreiber, C., Carley, K.M.: Going beyond the data: empirical validation leading to grounded theory. Comput Math Organ Theory **10**, 155–164 (2004)

Snijders, T.A.B., Steglich, C., Schweinberger, M.: Modeling the co-evolution of networks and behavior. In: Van Montfort, K., Oud, H., Satorra, A. (eds.) Longitudinal Models in the Behavioral and Related Sciences. Lawrence Erlbaum, Mahwah (in press)

Sorenson, O., Stuart, T.E.: Syndication networks and the spatial distribution of venture capital investments. Am. J. Sociol. **106**, 1546–1588 (2001)

Watts, D.J., Dodds, P.S., Newman, M.E.J.: Identity and search in social net-works. Science 17 **296**(5571), 1302–1305 May 2002

Wegner, D.M.: Transactive memory: a contemporary analysis of the group mind. In: Mullen, B., Goethals, G.R. (eds.) Theories of Group Behavior, pp. 185–205. Springer, New York (1986)

Chapter 3
Modeling and Simulating Command and Control for Naval Air Defense Operation

Keywords Naval air defense · Antiship missile · Defense modeling and simulation · Modeling and simulation · Battle experiment · Abstraction level · Modeling and simulation pyramid · Multi-resolution modeling · AEGIS · High-level architecture · Decision making

3.1 Introduction

This chapter introduces a case study of naval air defense whose mission is defending the fleet from an incoming swarm of antiship missiles.[1] Because the missiles approach in a high speed and in multiple directions, the fleet should coordinate its defense very responsively. At the same time, the missiles might strike the fleet in multiple separate waves, so the fleet commanders should carefully consider in using the ships and the on-board weapons for each wave of attacks. This situation is impossible to be replicated multiple times in the real world, so the defense modeling and simulation (DM&S), technique has been used. Moreover, DM&S has played an important role in the military for training, analysis, and acquisition (Piplani et al. 1994; Department of Defense 2006). For instance, DM&S is utilized to provide a virtual training environment to system operators and warfighters (Zavarelli et al. 2006); DM&S is applied to estimate the force depletion rate and the mission success probability (Cramer et al. 2008); and DM&S is developed to evaluate the effectiveness of weapon systems to be purchased (Manclark 2009). These various applications resulted in diverse DM&S systems with different objectives and at different abstraction levels (Harrison et al. 2002).

---

[1] This case study is initially published by Simulation: Transactions of the Society for Modeling and Simulation, International (Kim et al. 2012). This chapter expands the original article by expanding the model description and discussion in conjunction with the command and control research. Additionally, this chapter includes the discussion of utilizing formalism in the agent-based modeling to compare this case study to the case study presented in Chap. 2.

I.-C. Moon et al., *Modeling and Simulating Command and Control*,
SpringerBriefs in Computer Science, DOI: 10.1007/978-1-4471-5037-4_3,
© Il-Chul Moon 2013

To maximize the utilization of existing DM&S systems, the DM&S community has developed the interoperations between DM&S systems and has increased the usability of interoperating systems (RTO NATO Modeling and Simulation Group 2004). Along this venue of the interoperation research, the community has developed the standard and the protocols of M&S interoperations, which mainly focused on the technical feasibility of the interoperations. This effort resulted in the success of Simulation Interoperability Standards Organization (SISO) (SISO 2012); and high-level architecture (HLA) and run-time infrastructure (RTI) (IEEE Std 1516 2000; SAICTR Group 1999). One example of such interoperation usage is the simulation runs of multi-branch military exercises (Michael 1999; Maurice 2003).

Besides the technical development, this community is moving toward suggesting theoretic frameworks and motivation of interoperations. Particularly, this chapter hypothesizes that two heterogeneous levels of models can interoperate to generate emerging insights into a doctrine compared to standalone battle experiments. Currently, existing DM&S models are often limited to simulate a fixed number of variables related to a certain analysis index (Huntsville 2000), nevertheless the models might have overlapping variables. For instance, the naval air defense of a fleet can be modeled at different levels. A model may focus on the maneuver of missiles, the detailed operation of, and the warship behaviors (Ozkan et al. 2005; Lalis 2007). Another model may simulate the fleet formation, the command and control (C2) process, and the warship behaviors (Stevens et al. 1999; Calfee and Rowe 2004). Considering these two different models about the same situation, the models include the different factors of interest, the different abstraction levels of operations, the different details of the scenario inputs, and some overlapping variables (Davis 2000). Then, our research question is: what if we interoperate these two heterogeneous models of the same situation via the overlapping variables to perform a battle experiment? Furthermore, our question is whether the interoperation will yield new insights into the command and control that were not obtainable from two standalone models.

This case study presents a virtual battle experiment of the naval air defense through the interoperations of two heterogeneous models. The two models are the engagement- and the mission-level models that differ in the scenario, the behavior, and the analysis index details. Through this application, firstly and theoretically, we illustrate novel battle experiment framework via the interoperation of multiple heterogeneous levels of models, i.e., the semantic variable matching and the interoperation basis of heterogeneous models. Secondly and empirically, we show that the engagement-level model alone, the mission-level model alone, and the interoperation model of the two models produce statistically different insights into some modeled features of the battle experiments. For example, our interoperation experiment claims that there is an adequate amount of decision-making time for the naval air defense, while conventional command and control dictates that faster decision making is better in the defense. The contribution of our interoperation battle experiment is finding such new insight into the experimented command and control, which the insight is not obtainable from standalone battle experiment.

3.1.1 Previous Research

We review three areas of our study: the heterogeneous defense modeling levels, the utilization of multiple models, and the naval air defense models. Thus, we first argue where our mission and engagement-level models belong to in terms of the abstraction levels of DM&S. Then, we survey existing research issues in the multi-modeling area. Finally, we survey existing naval air defense models and their focuses.

3.1.2 Abstraction Levels of Defense Modeling and Simulation

The DM&S has various abstraction levels according to the modeling entities and scenarios of interests (Committee on Technology for Future Naval Forces 1997). Figure 3.1 organized these levels as the engineering, the engagement, the mission, and the campaign levels. These levels are different in modeled entities, scenarios, and resolutions. For instance, when we model the naval air defense situation, the modeled entities in the engineering level would be the propulsion, the guidance, the explosion systems of the air threats as well as the propulsion, the detection, the countermeasure systems of the friendly warships. On the contrary, the modeled entities in the mission level would be the formation, the fleet headquarter, the shared situation awareness of the air threats as well as the friendly warships. The element of command and control would be included in the engagement, the mission, and the theater-level models, yet we see that the mission-level models would have the finest details of the command and control. The engagement-level models are the small-sized combats, so the war-fighting skills would be more important issue than the large-scale command and control. Also, the theater-level

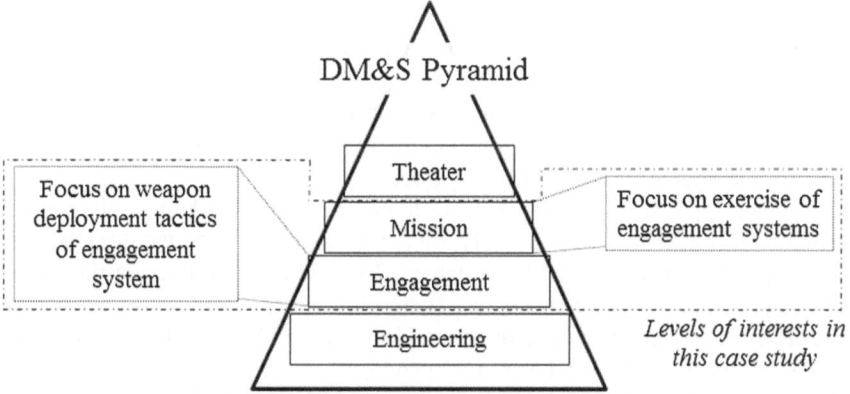

Fig. 3.1 Modeling and simulation pyramid for defense modeling and simulation

model might emphasize the command and control, but the resolution can be too low to model the specifics of the command and control. The mission-level models have several distinctions that focus on details of modeling command and control. First, the mission-level model is the model that focuses the whole stages of a single operation, so the model needs to describe the observation, the orientation, the decision making, and the action of the command and control. Second, the mission-level model often describes the units whose size requires the details descriptions of command and control. The company, the battalion, and the regiment level units require fine touch of command and control compared to either small sized unit, such as squad, or large-sized unit, such as army. We organized this simple comparison in Table 3.1. Through this comparison, we identified that the difference in modeling levels resulting in significant changes of overall model information and structure.

To our knowledge, one of the earliest formal introductions of these abstraction levels is introduced by Systems Acquisition Manager's Guide from U.S. military researchers (Piplani et al. 1994). The guide itemizes which levels of abstraction should concern which features, i.e., a campaign level model is focused on an Air-wing, a Corp or a Battle group; and an engineering-level model simulates fire control or radar. This guide clearly spells out why the field requires such distinct abstractions and what the models should concern at a certain abstraction level. Though this is limited to a practical guideline, researchers have developed theoretic discussion of the M&S pyramid in (Piplani et al. 1994; Davis and Hillestad 1993; Harrison et al. 2002).

3.1.3 Utilization of Multiple Models

In academia, researchers have utilized multiple models to better simulate and experiment a scenario (Fishwick et al. 1994; Levent et al. 2007). These models differ in the abstraction level, the modeling approach, and the modeling perspective. First, some multi-resolution modeling, or MRM, works utilize different models of different resolutions and interoperate the models to enable changing resolution levels (Davis 2005). The key technology of this type of MRM is aggregating and disaggregating simulated entities to apply a selected model with an appropriate resolution, and some used interoperation techniques when they perform the aggregation and the disaggregation.

Another type of multi-modeling is a multi-method modeling, or a hybrid modeling (Sung et al. 2009). Largely, modeling approaches are the discrete event based approach, i.e., the DEVS formalism (Bernard et al. 2000), and the continuous approach, i.e., system dynamics. These different approaches have advantages in different applications and resolutions. Hence, their interoperation to develop a hybrid approach model has been investigated.

Also, there is a case study of utilizing two models in a single battle experiment (Maurice 2003). This case study performs a simulation of one model and turns the

Table 3.1 Comparisons of engineering, engagement, mission, and theater-level models in the naval air defense

Comparison points	Engineering-level models	Engagement-level models	Mission-level models	Theater-level models
Modeled system	*Single or multiple weapon systems*: radar, missile, ship, etc.	*One-on-one combat situation*: a missile versus a warship	*Many-on-many combat situation*: a swarm of missiles versus a fleet of warships	*Strategic situation*: multiple fleet deployments to defend an operational theater
An example of modeling objectives	To find optimal system specifications	To find optimal weapon deployment tactics	To find better C2 activities and defense doctrines	To find better operational asset deployments and mission assignments
Modeled entities	Missiles, radar, and counter-measures	Warships, warship operators	Fleet commanders, fleet communication links	Support ships, naval bases, and strategic landmarks
Modeled command and control	None	Single ship command and control, no coordination between units	Multiple ship command and control, heavy emphasis on coordinated defense across fleet	Command and control between multiple fleets, less details on actual defense
Performance indicators	Speed, accuracy, and response time	Survival rate of a warship, interception rate of a missile	Fleet operational status	Number of strikes to strategic landmarks and naval bases
An example of battle experiment design	Precise performance comparisons to real-world systems	Comparisons between weapon deployment tactics	Comparisons between doctrines of fleet organization and operations	Comparisons between alternative strategic plans

simulation outputs into the simulation inputs of another model. This might not be an interoperation approach in a strict sense because the models were utilized in turn and off-line. Our interoperation approach adapts a feedback loop to this previous experiment through on-line interoperations. From the replications of one model with another model generated scenario, the input variable value is generated and provided to another model to continue the simulation.

3.1.4 Naval Air Defense Model

There are a number of mission-level simulation models focusing on naval air defense. Generally, the models include human behavior, such as that of radar operators, fleet commanders, and warship captains, which are required at the mission-level modeling. For instance, Carley and Lin developed a model named COPR to simulate a fleet commander's and radar operators' behaviors in naval air defense (Carley and Lin 1995). The model's objective was to evaluate a C2 structure encompassing a commander, mid-level officers, and radar operators. Hence, this model does not include any counter-measures or deployment tactics, yet the model illustrates a detailed air threat identification process. We regard this model as a combination of the engagement and the mission-level models, considering its in-depth modeling of human behavior, yet its lack of combat doctrinal attributes for multiple warships.

In a similar vein to Carley and Lin's work, Liebhaber and Smith introduced a computer simulator to experiment within a naval air defense situation (Liebhaber and Smith 2000). They mainly utilized the tool as a survey technique to observe the actual cognition processes of U.S. Navy air defense officers within the situation. Hence, this tool is categorized as a virtual simulation model while Carley and Lin's work is a constructive model generating estimations of performances for each fleet C2 structure. Additionally, Calfee adds an AEGIS Combat Information Center (CIC) simulation for the antiair situation (Calfee 2003). He modeled the CIC officers as agents and designed detailed response behavior mechanisms for the agents. He used the simulator to recreate the communication patterns, the decision-making processes, and the mental processes of the CIC officers. We follow the human behavior modeling of the previous mission-level models. However, the previous models often focused on the interactions within a CIC, a warship, or fleet headquarters and the models did not include warship behavior and counter-measure deployments.

3.2 Battle Experiment Scenario: Naval Air Defense

We apply our interoperation battle experiment framework to the naval air defense scenario and related doctrine. The naval air defense is a sequence of activities to make enemy warplanes and missiles ineffective or to reduce their threat level against friendly warships, and such sequence of activities are specified as the doctrine of naval air defense (Neary 2008). The defense of the warship is difficult mainly due to its geographical characteristics, e.g., no concealment against threats. To compensate for this difficulty, modern navies have developed antiair weapon systems, which resulted in the multi-layer defense concept. This concept assumes that many warships with various detection abilities defend themselves with respect to the distance of the threats by stages. The warship tries to mitigate threats from long distances to short distances, according to the ranges of various weapon systems on board. At the same time, the warships maintain a certain formation to optimize the opportunities to intercept the threats.

Finally, there is a central fleet headquarter situated either on one of the warships or in a distant place, and the headquarter is responsible for the overall command and control of the threat interceptions among the warships. In detail, there are two different levels of command and control. The first level is the fleet level, which are the intership command and control. Based upon the formation and the threat approach, each ship would be assigned to the defense of a certain direction. The command and control of this fleet-wise operation includes the fleet commander, the fleet combat staffs, and the warship commanders. The second level is the intra-ship command and control. Even a single vessel, there are numerous commanders and operators for each section: the weapon system, the radar system, the captain, etc. The warship commander, or the captain of the ship, receives the order from the fleet headquarter, and the commander utilize the ship's resources to follow the order. Particularly, in this scenario, the loop between the radar and the weapon system should be constantly monitored by officers and the commander.

Given the short description of the situation, we limit ourselves to model the below entities in the real world because modeling the complete situation is still a work-in-progress and because our intent is demonstrating the impacts of enabling interoperation battle experiments. The limitation is based on a doctrine of the Republic of Korea Navy. First, our simulation limits air threats to missiles, specifically. We assume that the missiles fly directly toward a warship. Then, we model on-board weapon systems with different capabilities in terms of detection and counter-measures. Lastly, we model the fleet command and control that imitates the fleet headquarters coordinating the warship operations.

It should be noted that we divided situation into two different levels and developed two corresponding models, see Figs. 3.2 and 3.3.

- Mission-level Doctrine in Fig. 3.2—There is a central fleet headquarter situated either on one of the warships or in a distant place. The headquarter commands the overall cooperation process of the threats interceptions among the warships, and the fleet command and control determines the number of threats against warships and hit when the threats are within a decision radius of the command and control.
- Engagement-level Doctrine in Fig. 3.3—Many warships defend themselves with respect to the distance of the threats by stages. The warships try to mitigate threats from long distances to short distances, according to the ranges of three

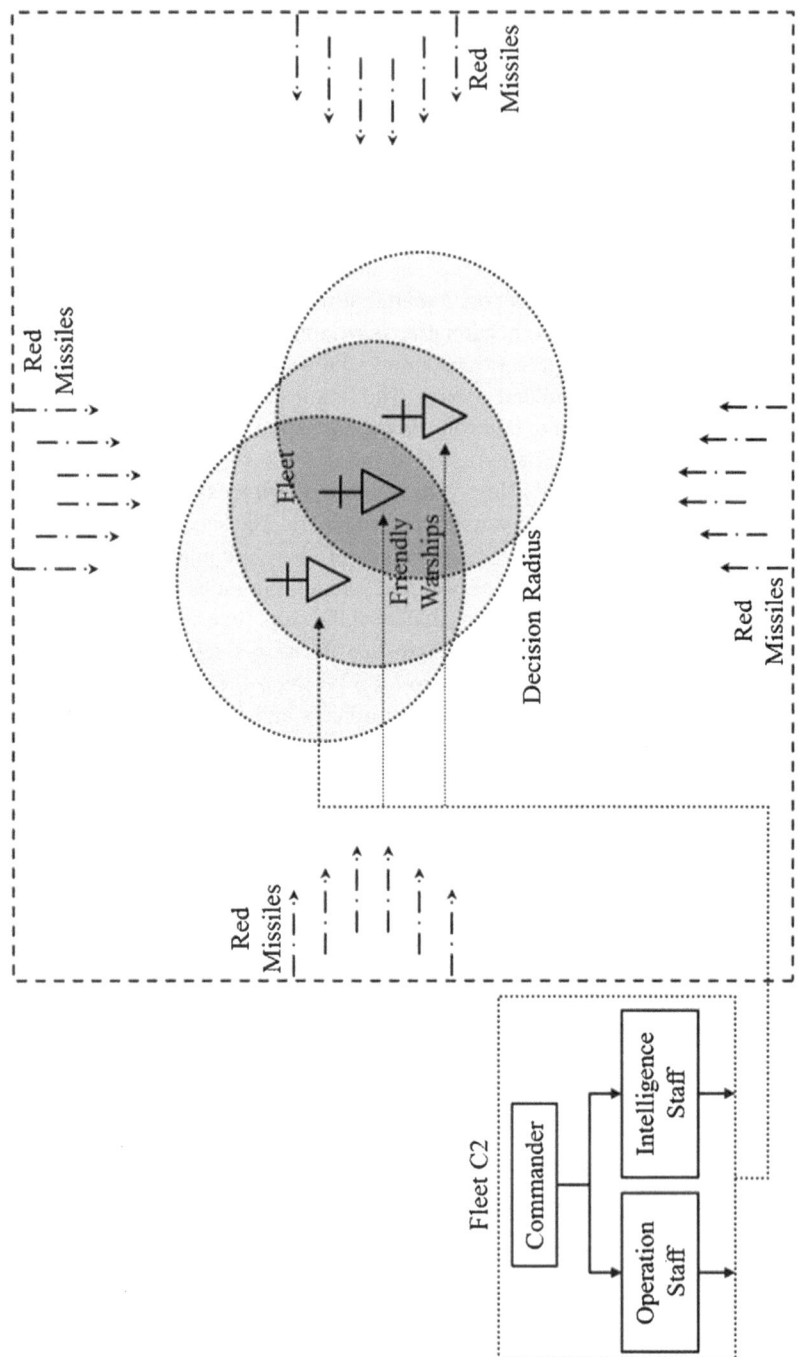

Fig. 3.2 Naval air defense scenario at the mission-level model, reconstructed from the mission-level doctrine

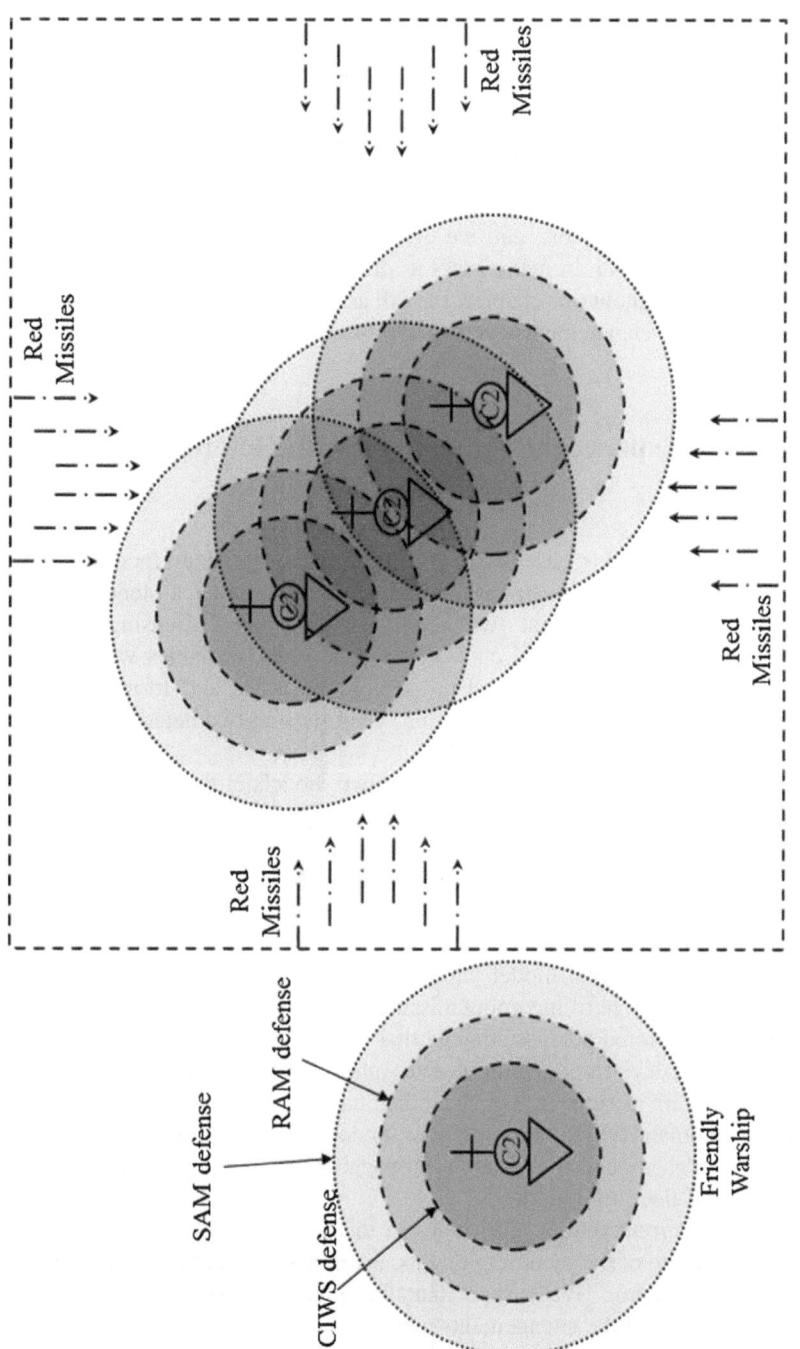

Fig. 3.3 Naval air defense scenario at the engagement-level model, reconstructed from the engagement-level doctrine

weapon systems, such as SAM, RAM, and CIWS, on board. The warship command and control operates its warship weapon system and radar system.

Often, when a situation is presented, modelers develop a single model according to the model objective. For instance, some may focus on the detailed operational behavior of a single warship against multiple air threats. Others may focus on the detailed command and control behavior of multiple warships with fewer details about the single warship operations. Then, the two perspectives will yield two different models, and we often see such diverse model developments from a single situation in many cases as discussed in the M&S pyramid works in the above. Throughout this chapter, we will assume that we have two models at the mission and the engagement levels of the M&S pyramid.

3.3 Battle Experiment Framework with Heterogeneous Models

The motivation of this case study is utilizing heterogeneous models to explore alternative battle experiment results compared to utilizing a standalone model. Particularly, we notice that two heterogeneous models focusing on different abstractions of command and control and with shared variables would be synergetic in the battle experiment. This section illustrates and formulates a battle experiment framework that exploits this synergy using two heterogeneous models of command and control.

In our naval air defense case, we have two models at the engagement and the mission levels. These models are able to perform battle experiments by itself at its own abstraction level. The difference of the experiments is their modeling focuses that the engagement-level model aims to simulate detailed weapon deployment behavior and the mission model concentrates on the command and control behavior of the fleet naval air defense. Because of this difference in the modeling focus, the mission-level model parameterizes the engagement procedures as an average intercept rate of incoming missiles. Additionally, the mission-level model simplifies the layered defense strategy that the engagement-level model simulates, so the mission-level model simply determines its missile hit when the missile is within a certain perimeter. On the other hand, the mission-level model has a detailed command and control structure model and its simulated decision-making time and engagement information propagations via communications between warships and fleet headquarters.

With the current setting, the values of the mission-level model variables, i.e., the intercept rate of the incoming threats, is provided by subject-matter experts, or rare historic records. We suspect that the engagement-level model with more detailed features of the engagements may produce the input values of the mission-level models dynamically, and this would provide new insights into the battle experiment. The following subsections illustrate the theoretic framework and the technical implementations of the parameter generations for input variables through the interoperations.

3.3.1 Theoretic Framework of Battle Experiments with Heterogeneous Models

To formulate the model interoperation, we start with the below expression of two different models with the same scenario, yet with different abstraction levels. Fundamentally, we treat a simulation model as a black-box function of an input variable set and an output variable set, see Formula 3.1.

$$O = M(I), \ V = I \cup O \qquad (3.1)$$

In Formula 3.1, O is the output variable set; I is the input variable set; and M is the model between O and I. Finally, V is the variable space that is the union of I and O of M models. We apply this expression to the mission model, M_M, and the engagement-level model, M_E, and we distinguish the models with the subscriptions of the expressions, see Formula 3.2 and 3.3.

$$O_M = M_M(I_M) \qquad (3.2)$$

$$O_E = M_E(I_E) \qquad (3.3)$$

Then, we investigate the relations between the variables of the two models. Since the two models are simulating the same scenario with different abstractions, we hypothesize that there are overlapping variables between V_M and V_E.

For further information of the variable overlapping, we display Fig. 3.4 and Table 3.2 describing which level of model abstractions focuses on which variables. Mainly, the mission and the engagement models share the representation of friendly deployments and opposition approaches as well as the basic specifications of friendly and opposition forces. Besides the overlapping variables, each model has its own focused variables, such as the decision-making time for the mission level and the radar search ratio for the engagement level. Under these expressions, our interoperation approach merges the two variable spaces. Formula 3.4 is the theoretic expression of the interoperating model.

$$O_{ME} = M_{ME}(I_{ME})$$
$$\text{when} \quad O_{ME} = (O_M \cup O_E) - (I_M \cup I_E) \qquad (3.4)$$
$$I_{ME} = I_M \cup I_E$$

Formula 3.4 specifies that the interoperation model produces outputs which are not the inputs of the interoperating models either. At the same time, the inputs are the union of all the inputs of the interoperating models. Having specified the inputs

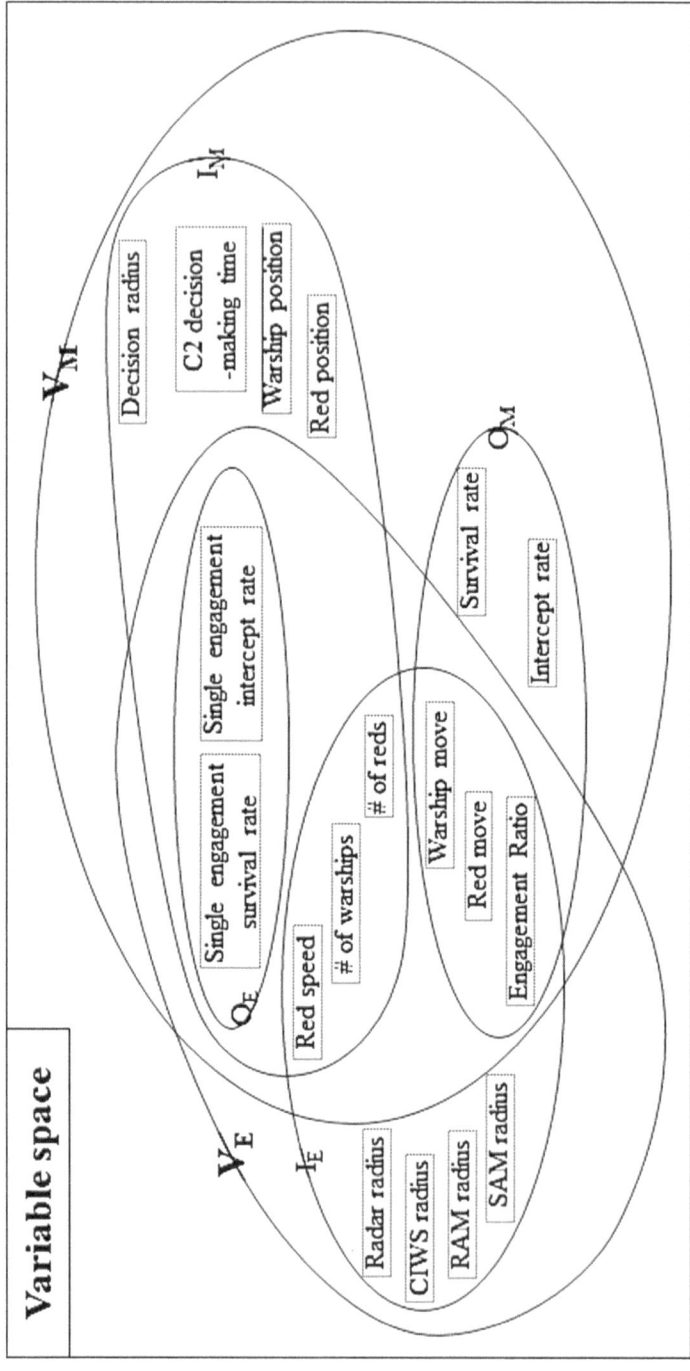

Fig. 3.4 Venn diagram for the variables of the engagement level and the mission-level models

Table 3.2 List of input and output variables of the mission level and engagement-level models

I_E	I_M	O_E	O_M	Name	Description
O	O			Number of warships	The number of warships composing fleet (default = 3)
O	O			Number of red missiles	The number of red missiles in the threat forces (varied in the experimental design)
	O			Warship position	The X, Y, and Z coordinates of warships composing fleet (warships' default coordinates = <150, 170 km>, <160, 170 km>, <170, 150 km>)
	O			Red missile position	The directions of red missiles in the threat forces. The red missiles are located in four directions relative to warships before engagement starts. For each direction, the number of red missiles is same (four default directions = North, West, East, South)
O		O		Warship move	The X, Y, and Z coordinates of warships generated from the engagement level
O		O		Red missile move	The X, Y, and Z coordinates of red missiles generated from the engagement level
O	O			Red missile speed	The missile speed of red missiles in the threat forces. The speed of all missiles is the same (varied in the experimental design)
O				RADAR radius	The maximum detection radius of RADAR on warship (default = 1,000 km)
O				CIWS radius	The maximum radius of SAM on warship (default = 3.2 km)
O				RAM radius	The maximum radius of RAM on warship (default = 10 km)
O				SAM radius	The maximum radius of SAM on warship (varied in the experimental design)
	O			C2 decision-making time	The C2 decision-making delay time (second) (varied in the experimental design)
	O			Decision radius of the warship	The maximum radius of engagement decision (varied in the experimental design)
		O		Survival probability of warhips	The ratio of the number of survival warships to the total number of warships when an interoperation simulation is terminated
		O		Intercept probability of the red missiles	The ratio of the number of intercept red missiles to the total number of red missiles when an interoperation simulation is terminated
	O		O	Single-engagement survival probability	The ratio of the number of survived warships to the total number of warships for N replications
	O		O	Single-engagement intercept probability	The ratio of the number of intercept missiles to the total number of missiles for N replications

and the outputs of the interoperation model, we look into the opportunity of the interoperation between the two models. The opportunity comes from the overlapping variable of the two models. Formula 3.5 and 3.6 show how we can interlink variable spaces of two models from the overlap.

$$O_M = M_M(I_M) = M_M(I_M \cup (I_M \cap O_E))$$
$$= M_M(I_M \cup M_E(I_E)) \quad \text{when } I_M \cap O_E \neq \phi \qquad (3.5)$$

$$O_E = M_E(I_E) = M_E(I_E \cup (I_E \cap O_M))$$
$$= M_E(I_E \cup M_M(I_M)) \quad \text{when } I_E \cap O_M \neq \phi \qquad (3.6)$$

The key is that the engagement level and the mission-level models have inputs which are outputs of the other model, so one model can utilize another model to generate inputs. Having said this, to see an impact generated from the engagement model result to the mission model result, Formula 3.5 and 3.6 also specify the necessary condition: there should be an engagement model output variable that is also a mission model input variable, and vice versa. The differences between the standalone execution and the interoperation execution inherently lie in the value generation for the overlapping variables. The standalone execution relies on pre-determined values that are rigid to the dynamic situation changes in the model execution. On the other hand, the interoperation execution dynamically generates needed values, in our case, O_E that is a part of I_M, via another model runs.

This variable space specifies which model utilizes what information. However, this does not tell how the models are utilizing the information, in other words, how M_{ME} is organized. We provide the model organization and process in the next section to illustrate M_{ME}.

3.3.2 Technical Implementation of Battle Experiments with Heterogeneous Models

We layered the engagement model below the mission model in the structure of the interoperation model, M_{ME}. Therefore, multiple engagement scenarios arise in a mission scenario. Hence, we evoke the engagement model with dynamically composed engagement scenarios as the mission model progresses with a single scenario. Given this general simulation process of M_{ME}, Fig. 3.5 describes our technical implementation approach for enabling battle experiments with two heterogeneous models. This technical implementation is designed within the presented theoretic framework. First, we start the simulation with the mission-level model until we recognize that threats and warships consist of an engagement group planned by the fleet command and control in the mission-level model. Previously, after constituting the engagement group, the survivals and the intercepts are determined by the preset values for input variables, such as the probability of warship survival and the probability of threat interception, where the variables belong $I_M \cap O_E$. To overcome this limitation, we dynamically generate the probability distribution by running the engagement-level model, which has more detailed descriptions on the weapon systems. From the replications of the engagement-level model with the mission-level generated scenario that is $I_E \cap O_M$, the input variable value is generated and provided to the mission-level model to continue the simulation. This variable feedback loop is implemented by utilizing the existing interoperation technique, HLA/RTI. Additionally, Fig. 3.6 presents the simulation flow of two interoperating models when the technical implementation in Fig. 3.5 is completed.

3.4 Mission-Level Naval Air Defense Model

This section presents the mission-level model of our interoperating battle experiment. Table 3.2 illustrates the modeling variables and entities of the mission-level model. Additionally, we describe the model with the DEVS formalism and the DEVS diagram (Kim et al. 2011); see the overall model structure in Fig. 3.7. Figure 3.7 is the DEVS coupled model diagram including the fleet command and control, the warships and the red missile models. The structure of the mission-level model is the sum of three submodels: the fleet command and control model, the warship models, and the air threats. This reflects the fact that a fleet is controlled by a commanding team located either on one of the warships or in a remote location; the commanding team sends instructions to and receives reports from the warships in the situation; and the air threats interact with the warships through interceptions and strikes. Given the importance of the fleet command and control, the DEVS coupled model of the fleet command and control is illustrated in Fig. 3.7.

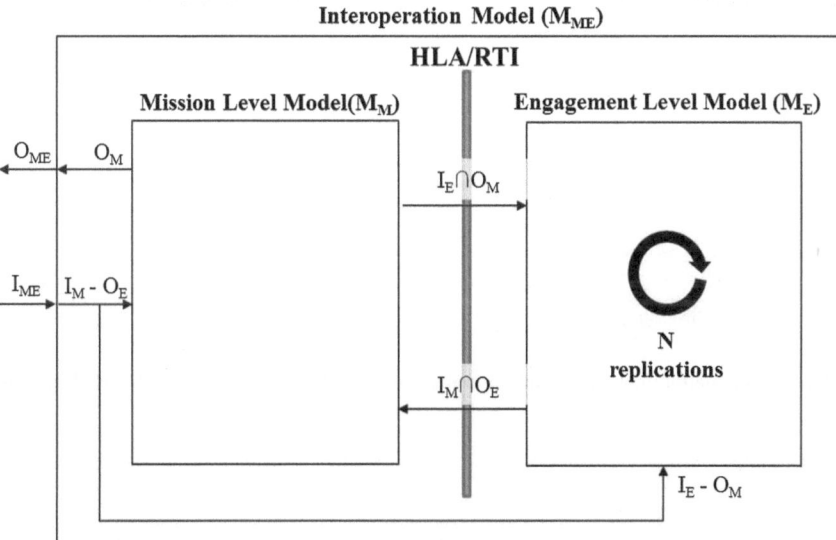

Fig. 3.5 Interoperation simulation process in technical implementation

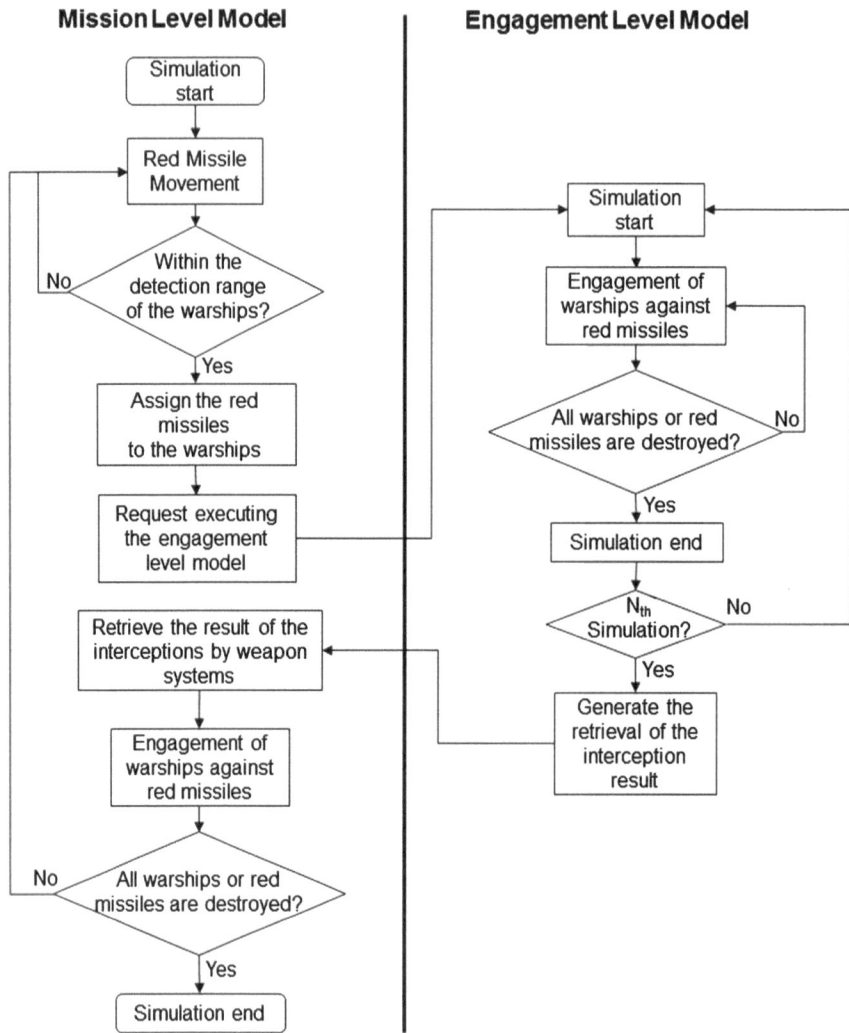

Fig. 3.6 Simulation flow of two interoperating models at different layers in the M&S pyramid

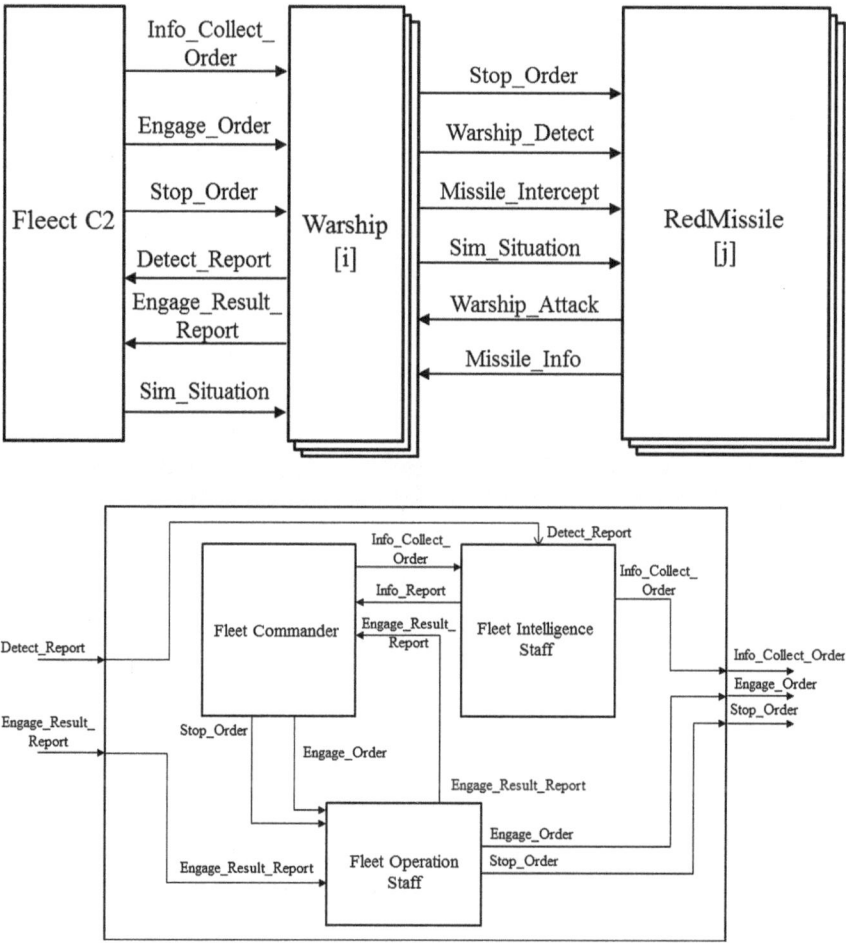

Fig. 3.7 (*Top*) DEVS coupling structure of the mission-level model (*Bottom*) DEVS coupling structure inside of the fleet command and control (C2) model

As Fig. 3.8 illustrated, these models follow the flow chart for many-to-many engagement. When multiple red missiles approach multiple warships, the fleet command and control receives red missile information coming from warships in the detection decision radius. The fleet command and control orders to each warship by assigning red missiles with the information, or Engagement Grouping. Once the assigned red missiles are in the fleet command and control decision radius, the grouped warships and red missiles engage. The accuracy rate of red missile and the weapon system of warship against red missile are fixed with default probability value, and our interoperation changes this as a dynamically fed variable. Finally, the intercept of red missiles and the survival of warships are

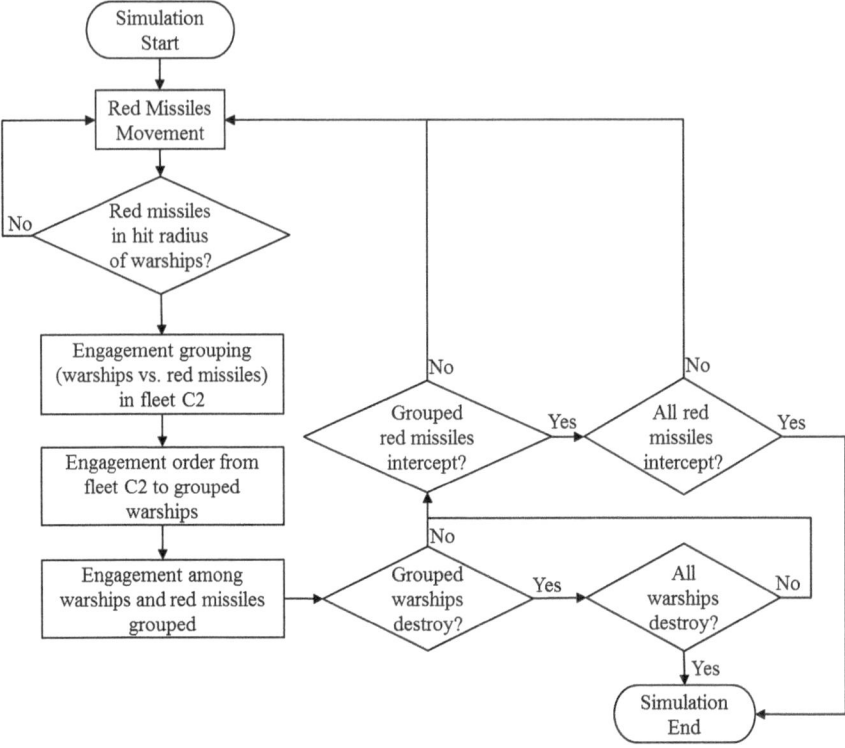

Fig. 3.8 Simulation flowchart of mission-level model

determined with the input variable value. Until either all warships are destroyed or all red missiles are intercepted, this simulation process will be continued.

3.5 Engagement-Level Naval Air Defense Model

While the engagement-level model does not contain any modeled entities about the fleet command and control and the fleet formation, the engagement-level model focuses more details of the individual warship command and control and weapon systems, and the air threats. The model objective at the engagement level is simulating the warship command and control process and the detailed weapon usage behaviors against threats.

As Fig. 3.3 and Table 3.2 illustrate, the engagement-level model concerns the warships and the red missiles. Before we further explain the details of the individual DEVS models, we show their couplings and the abstract structure of the overall model in Fig. 3.9. The structure of the engagement-level model is the sum of two submodels: the warship models and the red missile models. At the engagement level, warships are not controlled by a fleet C2 at a remote location. The objective of the engagement level is only to analyze effectiveness of warship combat system. Thus, the warship of the engagement level has more detailed entities of surface-to-air missile (SAM), rolling-airframe missile (RAM), closed-in weapon system (CIWS), and Radar. Given the importance of the warship, the DEVS coupled model of the warship is illustrated in Fig. 3.9, and its weapon system model in Fig. 3.9. Additionally, in Fig. 3.10, we display the atomic model of the warship commander in the warship command and control. The atomic model is the agent model that has the state transition by the perceived situation as well as the action performed.

The warship C2 sends instructions and receives reports collected with the equipment of warship; and the red missiles interact with the warships through interceptions and strikes. The engagement-level model follows the flowchart in Fig. 3.11. When multiple red missiles approach multiple warships, the warship C2 gets red missile information within the warship's detection radius. When red missiles are in fire ranges of SAM, RAM, and CIWS, the warship launches the countermeasures at a distance between the warship and the threat. In the order of longer fire ranges, one weapon system out of SAM, RAM, and CIWS is launched toward a threat. The weapon system selection is modeled by open documents (Department of the Navy 2007; Neary 2008) about navy weapon systems. The accuracy rate of individual warship weapon is fixed as the subject-matter expert suggested. The accuracy rate follows the below trend. The rate of the SAM has the highest value among other weapons, and the rate of the CIWS has the lowest value among other weapons. When a red missile is not intercepted by the CIWS of a warship, the warship is destroyed since the CIWS is the last countermeasure in terms of the fire range. The simulation procedure will be continued until either all warships or all red missiles are destroyed.

3.6 Battle Experiment Designs

We perform battle experiment with three models: (1) the standalone engagement-level model, or M_E; (2) the standalone mission-level model, or M_M; and (3) the interoperation model of the engagement and the mission model, or M_{ME}. The ultimate goal of this battle experiment is gaining new insights into existing doctrines by estimating the number of red missile intercepts and warship survivals of various scenarios. Therefore, we selected key variables in the doctrines that are already modeled in Fig. 3.4 and Table 3.2. To design battle experiments, we setup the independent variables of the experiments, or the scenarios. The experiment requires the models of weapon systems, C2 procedures, and fleet formations. However, M_E and M_M are specialized to modeling different systems and procedures, as described in Table 3.2. Hence, using the standalone model limits designing experiment variables in Table 3.3. On the other hand, the M_{ME} incorporates both variable spaces of M_E and M_M, so the M_{ME} provides the flexibility to

Table 3.3 Virtual battle experiment designs of the standalone engagement model, the standalone mission model, and the interoperation model, for each simulation case, we replicated for ten times

Experiment variable name	Experiment design of standalone engagement model, M_E	Experiment design of standalone mission model, M_M	Experiment design of interoperation model, M_{ME}	Implications
Number of red missiles (in I_E, I_M)	8, 16, or 24	8, 16, or 24	8, 16, or 24	Low, medium, or high level of air threats
Red missile speed (in I_E, I_M)	300, 480, or 680	300, 480, or 680	300, 480, or 680	Slow, medium, or fast speed of red missile
Missile interception radius of a warship (in I_E)	90,000, 110,000, or 130,000	Cannot design the experiment variable with M_M	90,000, 110,000, or 130,000	Short, medium, or long interception radius of warship
Decision radius of fleet C2 (in I_M)	Cannot design the experiment variable with M_E	90,000, 110,000, or 130,000	90,000, 110,000, or 130,000	Short, medium, or long decision radius of fleet C2
C2 decision-making delays (in I_M)	Cannot design the experiment variable with M_E	40, 50, or 60	40, 50, or 60	Fast, medium, or slow decision-making timings
Total number of battle experiment cells	27 cells (=3 × 3 × 3 cases)	81 cells (=3 × 3 × 3 × 3 cases)	243 cells (=3 × 3 × 3 × 3 × 3 cases)	Total number of battle experiment cells according to experiment variables

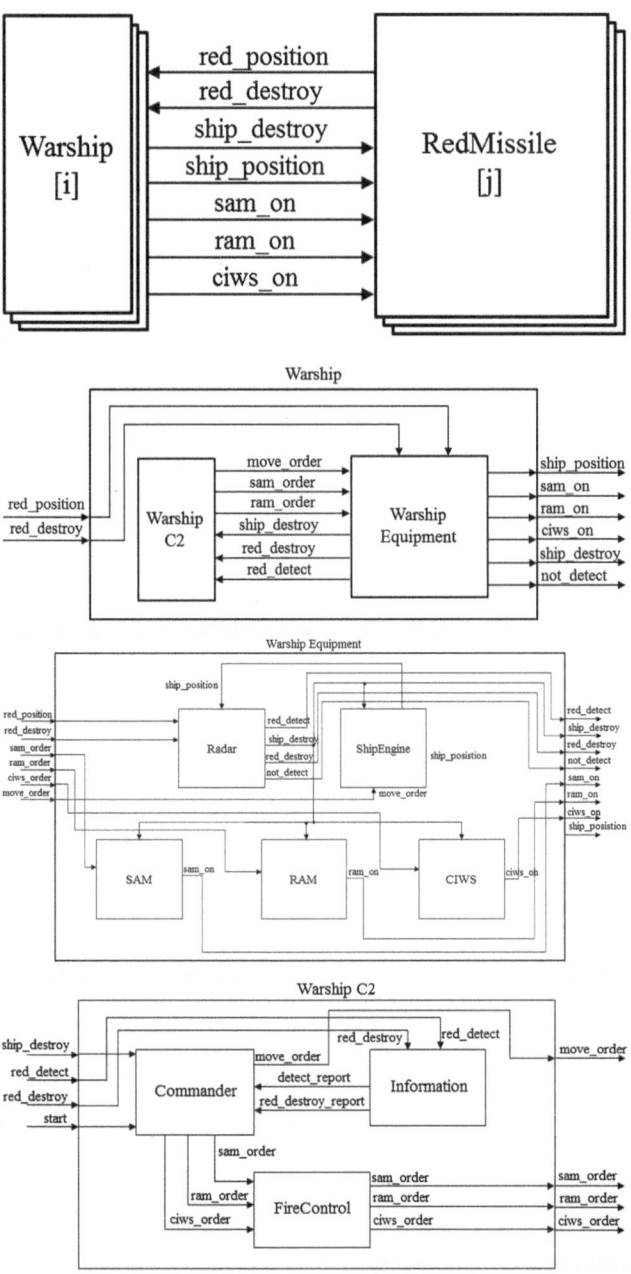

Fig. 3.9 (*First*) DEVS coupling model of engagement-level model, (*Second*) DEVS coupling model of the warship model inside the engagement-level model, (*Third*) DEVS coupling model of the warship equipment model inside the warship model, and (*Fourth*) DEVS coupling model of the warship command and control (C2) model inside the warship model

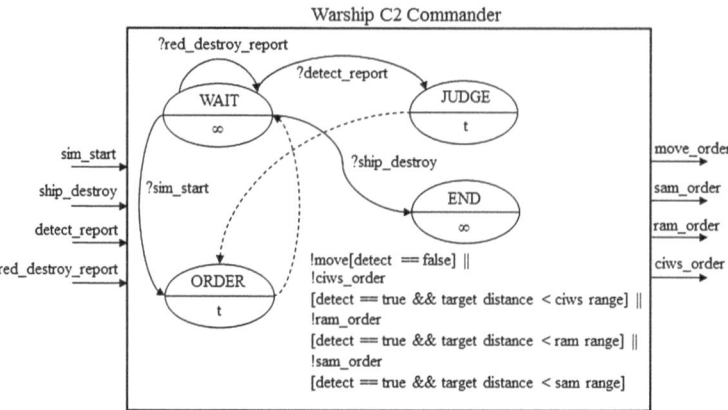

Fig. 3.10 State transition of the DEVS atomic model of warship commander in the warship command and control model

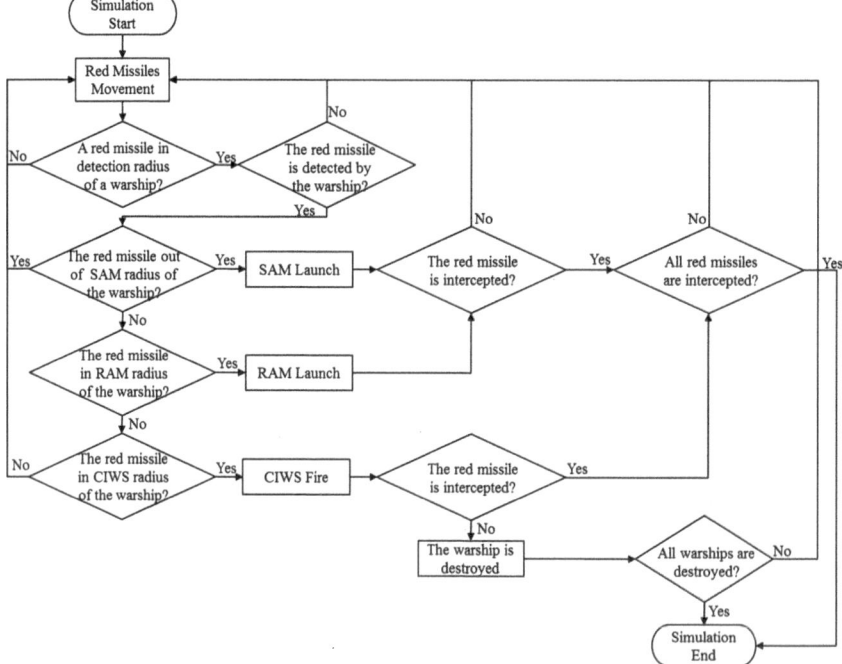

Fig. 3.11 Simulation flowchart of engagement-level model

design more complete experiment variables in Table 3.3, which is the value of our interoperating battle experiment framework.

When the independent experiment variables are designed as above, we design the dependent variable as the number of intercepts and survivals, in O_M, from the

Table 3.4 Standardized coefficient and adjusted R^2 from the meta-models by linear regression

Experiment variable name	Experiment design of standalone engagement model, M_E		Experiment design of standalone mission model, M_M		Experiment design of interoperation model, M_{ME}	
	Survival rate	Intercept rate	Survival rate	Intercept rate	Survival rate	Intercept rate
Number of red missiles (in I_E, I_M)	−0.679*	−0.613*	−0.271*	0.011	−0.421*	−0.513*
Speed of red missile (in I_E, I_M)	−0.567*	−0.645*	−0.476*	−0.524*	0.098*	0.057*
Missile interception radius of a warship (in I_E)	0.211*	0.237*			0.048*	0.084*
Decision radius of fleet C2 (in I_M)			0.291*	0.190*	0.110*	0.058*
C2 decision-making delays (in I_M)			−0.367*	−0.351*	0.112*	0.097*
Adj. R-square	0.803	0.827	0.517	0.431	0.212	0.285

*$P < 0.05$

three models. However, the engagement-level model does not model the rates at the fleet level because the model is limited to modeling engagements of a small number of warships. Therefore, we extrapolate the survival rate and the intercept rate in O_E of the engagement level to the number of survivals and intercepts in O_M of the mission level. The other models, the standalone mission-level model and the interoperation model directly provide the number of intercepts and survivals in O_M.

3.7 Battle Experiment Results

We describe battle experiment results in two ways. The first method is displaying the performance change trend by varying the independent experiment variable. This method can clearly visualize which factor influences which performance index either positively or negatively. The second method is building a meta-model of the battle experiment. With the visualizations alone, we cannot tell which factor is more sensitive and more robust than which factors. By examining the standardized coefficients and the P-values of the experiment variables of the meta-model, we can interpret the sensitivity and the robustness of the battle experiment result.

3.7.1 Trends of Battle Experiment Results

Figure 3.12 shows the performance changes from the three models, M_E, M_M, and M_{ME}, by varying the number of red missiles and the incoming speed of the missiles. Largely, the intercept and the survival rate decrease as the number of red missile and the incoming speed increase. One comparison point is the alignment of two standalone models. Because two models simulate different factors, the ranges of the results are different. For instance, the survival rate of the engagement-level model ranges from 0 to 100 %, but the same rate of the mission-level model ranges from 45 to 95 %. The range differences are identified in the other performance index. From our experiment design, due to the limits of the modeled variable spaces, both ranges are blind to the impact of the unconsidered factors. Then, our question is what would happen to the range when we increase the modeled variable space by using the interoperation model. The range from the interoperation model is from 0 to 45 %. This means that estimations of the survival and the intercept rate decrease significantly when we consider the whole variable space of the engagement and the mission-level models. On top of the range discrepancies, the trend discrepancy is more important. The range discrepancy can be resolved if we recalibrate the values of the experimental variables by each model. However, the trend discrepancy cannot be resolved by the variable calibration, i.e., the interoperation model shows that the low survival and the low intercept rates in the case of low incoming speeds.

The trend discrepancy of the interoperation model is explainable by two nonlinear influences from the interoperation. The first nonlinear influence is coming from the mission-level model to the engagement-level model. The engagement-level model receives an input variable, I_E, or the engagement ratio, which is generated as an output variable, O_M. The engagement ratio in Fig. 3.13 shows that the value trends of the mission-level model alone and the interoperation model are different due to the changes of an input variable, or the red missile speed. This first influence is caused by the second influence that will be discussed in the next paragraph.

The second nonlinear influence is coming from the engagement-level model to the mission-level model. The first influence is the changes of the engagement ratio. This engagement ratio causes the changed result of the engagement-level model outputs that is the single time engagement intercept rate, a variable in the intersection of I_M and O_E, see Fig. 3.14. This changed value is different from the predetermined input value in the mission-level model alone, which leads to different results between the mission-level model alone and the interoperation model when the value is fed back to the mission-level model in the interoperation.

We have not investigated fully which influence is the starter of this influence loop. This will require much sophisticated statistical study, and we will leave this research as a future work. However, we identified these interlocking influences between the two heterogeneous levels of models in the interoperation case, and

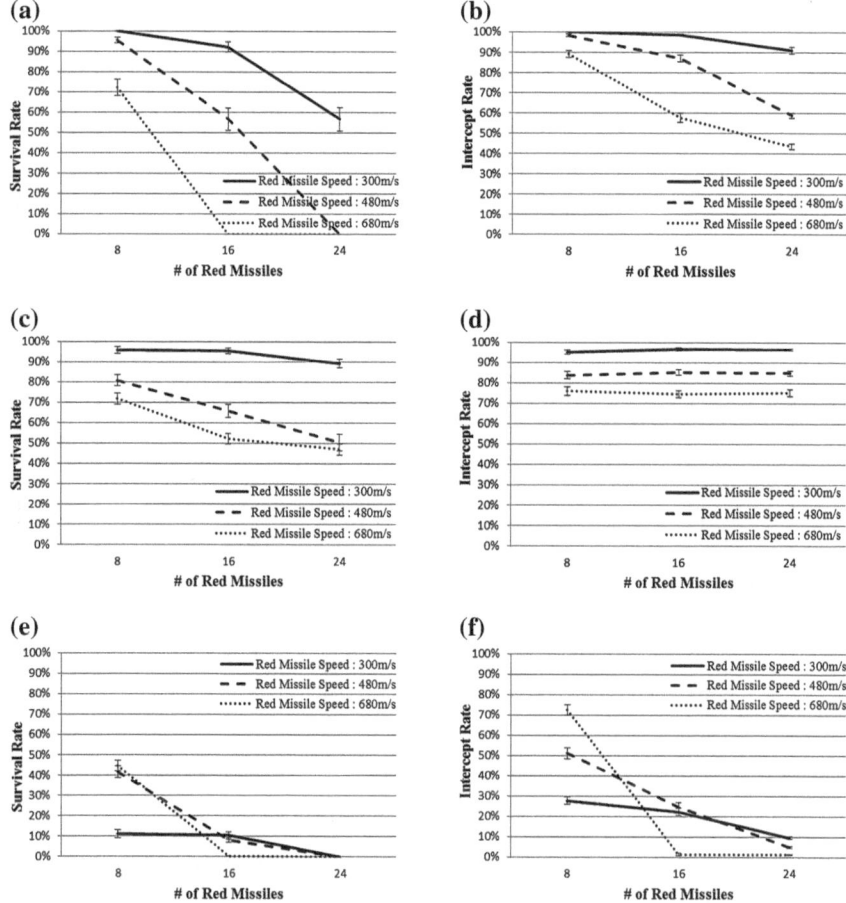

Fig. 3.12 Organizational performance over-time by varying the models of different layers at the M&S pyramid. **a** Survival rate of the standalone engagement model. **b** Intercept rate of the standalone engagement model. **c** Survival rate of the standalone mission model. **d** Intercept rate of the standalone mission model. **e** Survival rate of the interoperation model. **f** Intercept rate of the interoperation model

this is the true source of new insights coming from our proposed battle experiments via the simulation interoperation.

Such trend discrepancies are also found in interpreting other experiment variable. For example, the decision-making time is a factor of the mission-level model, and the factor describes how much time is needed to compose the engagement group by the fleet command and control. Generally, the shorter decision-making time makes the higher survival and the intercept rate, and this is supported by the standalone mission-level model, see Fig. 3.15. However, this estimation is only true when the single-engagement intercept rate is fixed as 20 %. As the decision-making time changes, the engagement ratio changes as well, see the illustration in

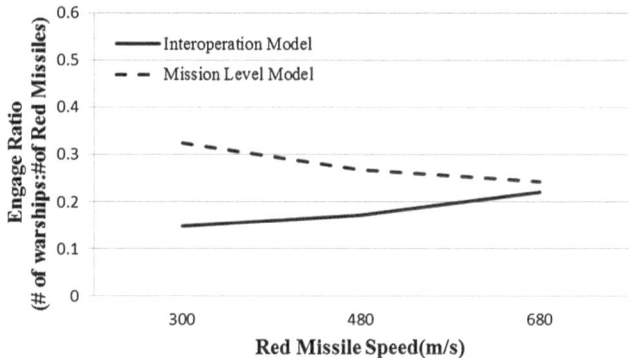

Fig. 3.13 Correlation between the red missile speed and the engagement ratio

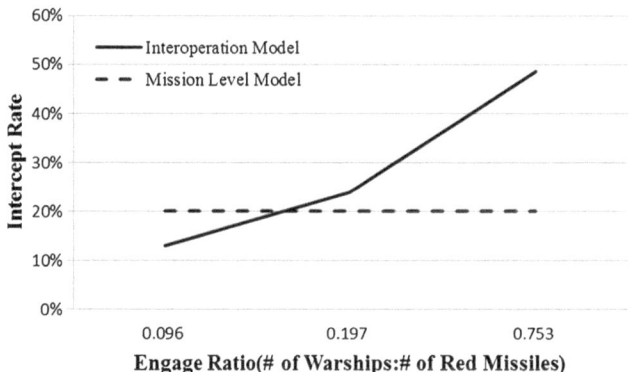

Fig. 3.14 Correlation between the engagement ratio and the intercept rate

Fig. 3.16. The figure shows that the ratio is the lowest when the decision-making time is 60 s for one engagement. Also, the lower engagement ratio makes the lower intercept rate. However, at the interoperation model, the intercept rate is the highest when the decision-making time is 50 s as Fig. 3.15 illustrated. The average engagement ratio for whole experiment cells at the time 50 is higher than 40 and 60 s because the two values (40, 60) have a higher number of engagement. The smaller number of red missiles makes the higher intercept rate, nevertheless the time 40 will have more the number of engagement than the time 50 since the number of red missiles in the decision radius are smaller than the time 50. The time 60 that has the number of red missiles in the decision radius is higher than the time 50, nevertheless the single-engagement intercept rate is lower than the time 50. Thus, the time 60 has higher the number of engagement than the time 50 since a number of survived red missiles will be higher than the time 50. Then, the engagement ratio changes impact the single-engagement intercept rates diverging from 20 %. Thus, the interoperation model yields a new insight that there is an

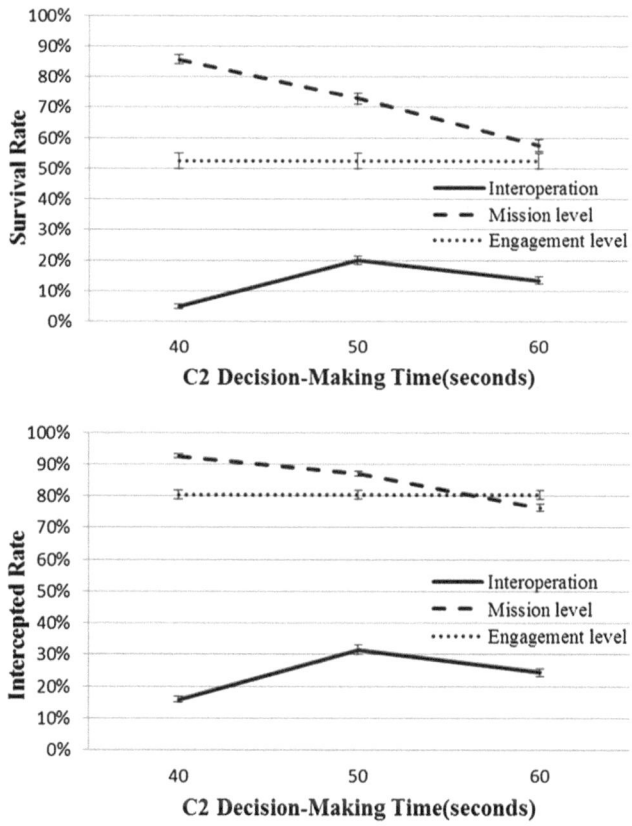

Fig. 3.15 Survival and intercept rate of the standalone models and the interoperation model by a command and control parameter, the decision-making cycle

optimal decision-making time, 50 s in our calibration, which results in an optimal engagement ratio which results in an optimal single-engagement intercept rate.

3.7.2 Meta-Models of Battle Experiment Results

This section statistically analyzes which factors are contributing which performance index how strongly and how robustly they are contributing to it. We build three meta-models for three battle experiment results from three models, M_E, M_M, and M_{ME}. The meta-model is a linear regression model with standardized coefficients and p-values for independent experiment variables against performance indexes, see Table 3.4. From the meta-models, we identify four major interpretations. The first finding is the decrease of the adjusted R-square as the model deals with more factors, particularly human-related factors. From the survival rate

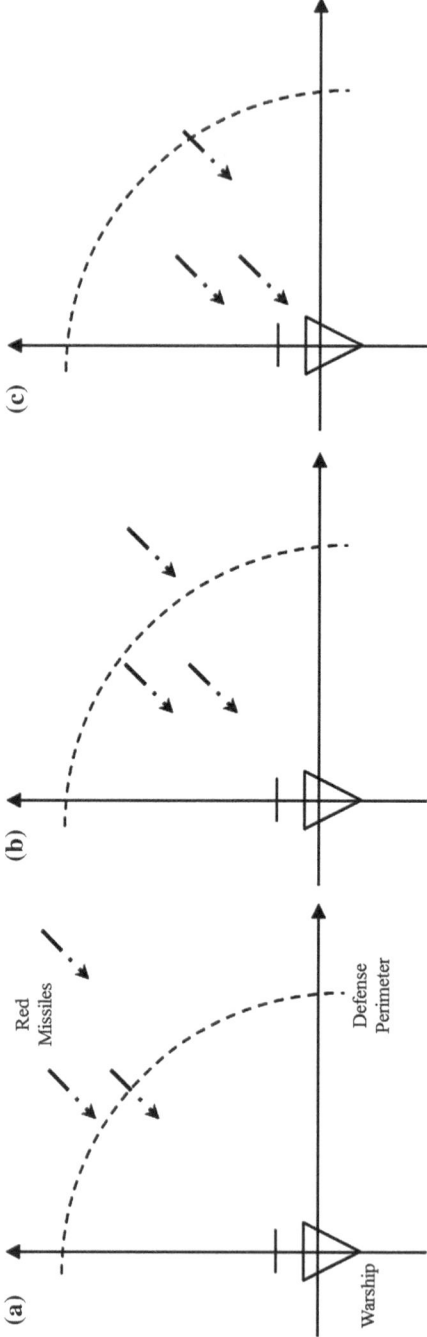

Fig. 3.16 Illustration of how the engagement ratio changes by the decision-making time at the command and control stage. **a** Delay time: 40. Too early judgement with partial information. **b** Delay time: 50 Right timing with full information. **c** Delay time: 60 too late judgement with full information

perspective, the adjusted R-square from the standalone engagement-level model, the standalone mission-level model, and the interoperation model reach 80.3, 51.6, and 21.2 %, correspondingly. This does not necessarily mean that the interoperation level model is unstable or less accuracy, rather this should be interpreted as the interoperation model is more complex and difficult to be explained by a linear model.

The second finding is the high standardized coefficient of the number of red missiles. The high coefficient means that the factor contributes more than the other factors. The increase of the number of red missiles contributes the increase of the survival rate in the interoperation model by 0.420 negatively. The increase of the command and control decision-making time contributes 0.112 positively in the same setting. From this sense, the number of red missiles contributes 3.76 times more than the command and control decision-making time in the survival rate. Similarly, we can compare the level of significances of factors in the experiments.

The third finding is the changing contributions of some experiment variables. When we look into the standardized coefficients of the decision-making time in the survival rate, the standalone mission-level model has -0.367; and the interoperation model has 0.112. The standalone mission-level model emphasizes the shorter decision-making time as we examine in the previous section, and this is confirmed by the high negative coefficient value. Nevertheless, the interoperation model shows that there is an optimal decision-making time, and this is confirmed by the low positive coefficient value.

The final finding is the table design itself. When we only utilize the standalone models, we cannot compare the significances of factors at different military levels. For instance, we may want to equip better a radar system to increase the missile interception radius. On the other hand, we may train our command and control personnel better to reduce the command and control decision-making time. These two factors are at different levels of military branches, yet we need to compare which is more significant in the overall naval air defense operation. This framework enables such comparison by interoperating heterogeneous levels of models.

3.8 Lessons Learned to Model and Simulate Command and Control

Command and control is not limited to the top commanders of a force. At every level of the force, such as fleet headquarter, squadron commander, warship commander, etc., there are commanding officer that executes the command and control activity. However, the simulation models are often designed to focus on a particular level of command and control, so the other levels of command and control are not modeled, or the levels are modeled as simple parameters. This simplification is unavoidable to a certain extent because of the nature of modeling process. However, this simplification also limits findings from modeling and simulating command and control. This case study points out such limitation of utilizing a single simulation model for studying command and control.

In detail, the focus of this case study is reporting the new insights into a naval air defense doctrine from interoperating two existing heterogeneous level models. Particularly, the insights are gained from the simulation-based battle experiment of the naval air defense operation. We used two models at the mission and the engagement levels. While the objective of the engagement-level model and doctrine is to find optimal deployment of combat system and weapon, the objective of the mission-level model and doctrine is to find better command and control activities. When the two models are both limited to their own modeled worlds, the insights from battle experiments using the models in the standalone manner are limited to the model concepts as well. However, the result of real-world battles is susceptible to the factors at the mission level as well as the engagement level. Hence, limited insights from the limited models may not show comprehensive estimations. Therefore, we need to extend the insight by merging the two modeled worlds into a single model world. To realize this battle experiment concept, we utilize the simulation interoperations, and we explain this battle experiment framework by the theoretic grounding as well as the empirical experiments. After our experiments, the framework demonstrates such new findings, i.e., a new insight into setting the command and control decision-making timing considering both engagement and mission-level factors.

It should be noted that the intention of this chapter is not accurately predicting the battle results though we think the proposed framework will contribute to the improvement of accuracy in the long term. Still, the accuracy will be largely determined by the accuracy of individual models merged into the interoperations. We limit our contribution to the extension of the battle experiment designs.

In spite of its limitation, our contribution is finding new insights into the naval air defense doctrine that are not obtainable from standalone model battle experiment. This finding is enabled by our battle experiment framework taking advantages of simulation interoperation. We expect that this work will provide a new methodology for battle experiments with dynamically changing and unobtainable variables.

References

Bernard, P.Z., Herbert, P., Kim, T.G.: Theory of modeling and simulation, 2nd edn. Academic Press, New York (2000)

Calfee, S.H.: Autonomous agent-based simulation of an AEGIS cruiser combat information center performing battle group air-defense commander operations. M.S. Thesis, Naval Postgraduate School (2003)

Calfee, S.H., Rowe, N.C.: Multi-agent simulation of human behavior in naval air defense. Naval Eng. J. **116**(4), 53–64 (2004)

Carley, K.M., Lin, Z.: Organizational designs suited to high performance under stress. IEEE Trans. Syst. Man Cybern. **25**(2), 221–230 (1995)

Committee on Technology for Future Naval Forces, National Research Council: Creating and improving intellectual and technological infrastructure for M&S. Technology for the United States navy and marine corps, 2000–2035: becoming a 21st-century force: vol. 9: modeling and simulation. National Academy of Sciences. Chap. 6, pp. 70–90 (1997)

Cramer, M.A., Beach, J.E., Mazzuchi, T.A., Sarkani, S.: Understanding information uncertainty within the context of a net-centric data model: a mine warfare example. 13th ICCRT. Paper: I-203 (2008)

Davis, P.K.: Exploratory analysis enabled by multiresolution, multiperspective modeling. In: 2000 Winter Simulation Conference, vol. 1, pp. 293–302 (2000)

Davis, P.K.: Introduction to multiresolution, multiperspective modeling (MRMPM) and exploratory analysis. Working paper. RAND (2005)

Davis, P. K., Hillestad, R.: Families of models that cross levels of resolution: issues for design, calibration and management. In: Proceedings of the 25th Conference on Winter Simulation, pp. 1003–1012 (1993)

Department of Defense, Office of the Under Secretary of Defense for Acquisition, Technology and Logistics: Acquisition modeling and simulation master plan. Systems Engineering Forum (2006)

Department of the Navy: Sea power for a new era 2007, a program guide to the U.S. Navy. http://www.navy.mil/policy/seapower/spne07/to-spone07.html (2007)

Fishwick, P.A., Hari, N., Jon, S., Andrea, B.: A multimodel approach to reason-ing and simulation. IEEE Trans. Syst. Man Cybern. **24**, 1433–1449 (1994)

Harrison, N., Gilbert, B., Lauzon, M., Jeffrey, A., Lalancette, C., Lestage, R., Morin, A.: A M&S process to achieve reusability and interoperability. In: RTO NMSG Conference (2002)

Huntsville: EADSIM execute summary. http://www.eadsim.com. Teledyne Brown Engineering, INC, Alabama (2000)

IEEE Std 1516: IEEE standard for modeling and simulation (M&S) high level architecture (HLA)—framework and rules (2000)

Kim, T.G., Sung, C.H., Hong, S-.Y., Hong, J.H., Choi, C.B., Kim, J.H., Seo, K.M., Bae, J.W.: DEVSim++ toolset for defense modeling and simulation and interoperation. J. Defense Model. Simul. Appl. Methodol. Technol. **8**(3), 129–142, July (2011)

Kim, J., Moon, I. C., Kim, T.G.: New insight into doctrine via simulation interoperation of heterogeneous levels of models in battle experimentation. Simul. Trans. Soc. Model. Simul. Int. **88**(6), 649–667 (2012)

Lalis, V.: Exploring naval tactics with UAVs in an Island complex using agent-based simulation. M.S. Thesis, Naval Postgraduate School (2007)

Levent, Y., Alvin, L., Simon, B., Tuncer, Ö.: Requirements and design principles for multiresolution, multistage multimodels. In: Henderson, S.G., Biller, B., Hsieh, M.-H., Shortle, J., Tew, J.D., Barton, R.R. (eds.) Proceedings of the 2007 Winter Simulation Conference, pp. 823-832 (2007)

Liebhaber, M.J., Smith, C.A.P.: Naval air defense threat assessment: cognitive factors and model. In: Command and Control Research and Technology Symposium (2000)

Manclark, J.: Air force test and evaluation presentation. U.S. Air Force T&E Days 2009 (2009)

Maurice, A.: Assessing the treatment of airborne tactical high energy lasers in combat simulations. M.S. Thesis, Air Force Institute of Technology (2003)

Michael, R.H.: Using army force-on-force simulations to stimulate C4I systems for testing and experimentation. In: Command and Control Research and Technology Symposium, ICCRTS. Paper: I-077 (1999)

Neary, C.J.: Navy surface tactical missiles. In: AIAA Strategic and Tactical Missile Systems Conference. Unclassified Presentation (2008)

OzKan, B., Rowe, N.C., Carfee, S.H., Hiles, J.E.: Three simulation models of naval air defense. 10th ICCRTS. Paper:I-194 (2005)

Piplani, L.K., Mercer, J.G., Roop, R.O.: Systems acquisition manager's guide for the use of models and simulations. Report of the DSMC 1993–1994. Defense Systems Management College, Fort Belvoir, Virginia (1994)

RTO NATO Modeling and Simulation Group (NMSG): M&S support to assessment of extended air defence C2 interoperability. RTO technical report (2004)

SAICTR Group: High level architecture run-time infrastructure RTI 1.3-next generation programmer's guide version 5. DMSO (1999)

Simulation Interoperability Standards Organization: http://www.sisostds.org/ (2012)

Stevens, W.K., Decker, W.L., Gagnon, C.M.: Representation of command and control (C2) and information operations (IO) in military simulations. In: Proceedings of the NATO Studies, Analysis and Simulation Panel (SAS) 1999 Symposium on Modeling and Analysis of Command and Control (1999)

Sung, C.H., Hong, J.H., Kim, T.G.: Interoperation of DEVS models and differential equation models using HLA/RTI: hybrid simulation of engineering and engagement level models. In: 2009 Spring Simulation Multi Conference (2009)

Zavarelli, J., De Chiaro, S. A., Fournier, J., Schweickert, D.A., Zislin, A.: Live virtual constructive experiments for C2 evaluation. 11th ICCRTS. Paper: I-090 (2006)

Chapter 4
Modeling and Simulating Command and Control for Disaster Response

Keywords Disaster response · Disaster management · Hurricane katrina · Virtual experiment · Network-centric operation · Network-centric warfare · Shared situation awareness · Synchronized action

4.1 Introduction

This case study presents the command and control of disaster response.[1] Many devastating disasters occurred in 2011, and some of the devastating damage could have been avoided if we managed the crisis better. For example, the Japanese disasters of earthquake and tsunami resulted in a near-meltdown of a nuclear reactor as well as the evacuation of tens of thousands of people (Matanle 2011). Although earthquakes and tsunamis are unavoidable natural disasters, the meltdown could have been avoided if the decision makers were provided with the right information at the right time. Similarly, the evacuees would have been better supplied if relief organizations were informed effectively. Similar incidents of information sharing problems were found in the New Zealand earthquake (Beavan et al. 2011) and the Seoul storm and landslides (Lee and Jung 2011). Considering these examples of crisis management, we are motivated to investigate the structures and the operations of command and control between organizations in the disaster management.

To investigate the command and control in the disaster management, we model and simulate the behavior of the organizations involved. Through the modeling and simulation, we virtually experimented with the efficiency and effectiveness of how the organizations operate and, more importantly, how the organizations are structured from the perspective of command and control. This case study introduces the details of our models, simulations, and virtual experiments. The dataset is the records of radio communications between relief organizations during the

---

[1] This case study is presented at the SCS Spring Multi-Simulation conference (Lee et al. 2012), and the study is not formally published as an article by any journal.

I.-C. Moon et al., *Modeling and Simulating Command and Control*, SpringerBriefs in Computer Science, DOI: 10.1007/978-1-4471-5037-4_4,

Hurricane Katrina disaster in 2005. These communications are the most inclusive record of the crisis operations (Comfort et al. 2010). We are in the process of collecting the datasets on other recent disasters such as the Japanese earthquake and tsunami and the Seoul landslides; we used the Katrina dataset to evaluate our modeling and simulation approach prior to finishing the data collection.

Our modeling approach is twofold: modeling organizational operations as agents and modeling an organizational structure as a network of organizations (Oh and Moon 2008). Particularly, our models focus on the network-centric operations of the relief organizations. The network-centric operations are the operations taking advantages from better information sharing from a carefully designed network of organizations (Lubitz et al. 2008). We apply this network-centric operation paradigm to the operations of the relief organizations, and we measure the degree of shared information (Oomes 2004) and the synchronization of actions through the information (Quijada 2006). This concept of the network-centric operation is well spread in the command and control of the military domain, yet civilian applications are under research and development. Our initial review suggests that there have been a few examples of agent-based models in the disaster management domain from the network-centric operation perspective.

We simulated the modeled agents and network by varying behavior parameters and network structures to find the impacts of those variations on information sharing. Our initial results using the dataset seemed to indicate when the organizational structure became most efficient at information sharing and the characteristics of the structure at the moment of best efficiency. Furthermore, we reviewed each organization's level of information sharing when the behavior parameters and the structures were differentiated. These analyses on information sharing and organizational structure answer the questions of how to manage relief organizations in crisis situations like the recent disasters from a network-centric operations viewpoint.

4.2 Previous Research

We reviewed the previous works in two dimensions. First, we surveyed the analyses of the situation from a methodological standpoint. The Katrina case is analyzed in many papers, and we found distinctions in our approaches from the previous works. Second, we reviewed the previous works on the network-centric operation because it is the major component in our analysis approach.

4.2.1 Analysis of Crisis Management Organizations

In the crisis management domain, the analysis of the collaborative and networked operations is one of the most frequently recurring research topics. The operations are analyzed at the individual, the intraorganization, and the interorganization levels. Also, the operations are analyzed based upon qualitative evaluations; quantitative, yet static evaluations; and quantitative and dynamic evaluations.

Many crisis management practitioners and researchers start their analyses from the qualitative approach. For instance, Comfort provided systematically organized qualitative evaluations of organizations in crisis management (Comfort 2007). She enumerated the key concepts, i.e., cognition, communication, collaboration, and control in the qualitative evaluations, and she argued how past crises were handled from the perspective of such concepts. In the medical field, Carl et al. said that the new policy for medical disaster response is more effective and could reduce immediate mortality after a severe disaster (Schultz et al. 1996). In public administration fields, Waugh and Streib (2006) said collaboration is important to treat natural and man-made crises, so we need new leadership that derive their power from effective strategies and compelling vision.

Often, the above qualitative analyses are supported by quantitative analyses from real-world observations. For instance, Comfort et al. (2010) strengthened their previous qualitative analyses with observations about the Katrina crisis management dataset. They counted the communication messages and coordinated efforts from the field survey, and they found the rates of successful responses to various requests and the bottlenecks of the responses in the process. By statistically examining the propositions from the real-world data, they qualitatively argued how to prepare organizations to behave resiliently. Bharosa et al. (2009) said sharing information is important, so they showed correlations among each level of factor—community, agency, and individual—using empirical analysis.

Finally, some researchers analyzed crisis management operations by utilizing the modeling and simulation approach. Oh and Moon showed how to utilize an agent-based model to find a new organizational structure for effective request and response handling (Oh and Moon 2008). They varied the organizational structure parameters as well as the organizational information process capacity. Their conclusion was introducing more links to the structure might not be a better solution than a capacity increase, because more links might induce more broadcasts of unnecessary information to organizations.

4.2.2 Network-Centric Operation in Crisis Management

As many practitioners and researchers pointed out that organizational structure and process is important in crisis management, some researchers approached this problem as the sort of command and control problem that is commonly discussed in the military domain (Alberts and Hayes 2006). In the early 2000s, researchers started a discussion on crisis management in the command and control framework. Rosen et al. (2002) discussed how to manage medical crises through futuristic command and control practices. Oomes (2004) discussed the importance of organizing command posts and the command and control structure to dynamically handle crises. Smith discussed that previous experiences provide an opportunity to collect information that would offer an enhanced perceptive of command and control of large-scale multiagency crisis response operations. Therefore, he conducted a phenomenological study about seven themes: experience, trust, preparedness, organization, leadership, strategic intent/vision, and communication (Smith 2010). However, these discussions had not been theoretically grounded until the introduction of network-centric operations.

After the introduction of network-centric warfare in the military (Alberts and Hayes 2003), the concept evolved to network-centric operations and was applied to civilian domains such as crisis management. Moffat (2008) applied the network-centric operation concept to the Katrina case, and he assessed the maturity of the organizational operations qualitatively. His major contribution was how to transform the military-style maturity assessment criteria to the civilian case. Another example of applying the network-centric operation concept is the hybrid simulation designed to evaluate the network-centric decision-making by Quijada (2006). By looking into the federal report, he captured the major points of modeling and simulating the crisis management organizations. His major modeling features include information/resource flows, disaster planning, communication systems, situation awareness, interoperability, human factors, and the chain of command.

We modeled selected features from the above in our simulations. In the selection process, we identify key factors in the network-centric operation, and the factors and their relations are enumerated in Fig. 4.1. However, we could find few publications elaborating the above model and the simulation results in the crisis management field from the network-centric viewpoint which we provide throughout this case study. From the survey of the previous works, we learned that the concept of the network-centric operation is still evolving to be applied to the crisis management domain. Yet, there is a lack of publications presenting the evolved concept in crisis management through detailed models and simulation results.

4.3 Methods

Our modeling and simulation focus on the operations and the structure of relief organizations in a crisis from the network-centric operations perspective. This section introduces the dataset, the intraorganizational model, the interorganizational model, and the analysis metrics from the network-centric operations. After introducing our models and analysis metrics, we show our virtual experiment design to test the efficiency of the crisis management operations in the dataset.

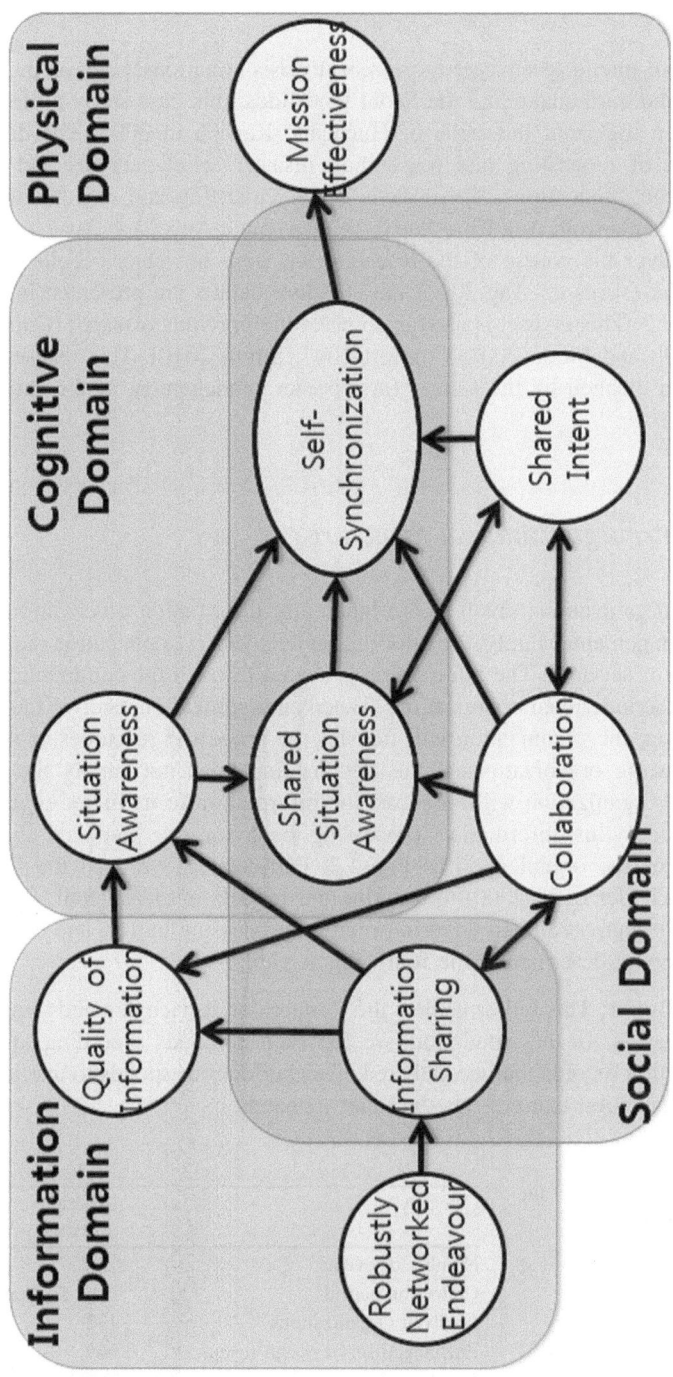

Fig. 4.1 Network-centric operation and its key factors in different domains

4.3.1 Dataset

Though we intend to analyze more recent crisis situations, such as the Japanese tsunami and earthquake and the Seoul landslides, this case study utilizes a communication log from the crisis of Hurricane Katrina in 2005. The dataset is a collection of requesting and responding disaster relief services and resources through communications. There were 2,227 requesting and responding communication events from Aug 27 to Sep 6. We designate Aug 27 as day 1 and Sep 6 as day 11. Over the course of the research, we were not able to collect the communication events on Aug 30, or day 4. More details are presented in Table 4.1 and Fig. 4.2. This dataset is used in some of the previous research (Comfort et al. (2010); Oh and Moon 2008; Comfort 2007; Smith 2010). This dataset was collected and cleaned by the Center for Disaster Management at the University of Pittsburgh.

4.3.2 Intraorganizational Structure

The 172 organizations involved are inherently information processing entities in crisis management. Mainly, the information tells which organization requires what resources or services. The information is shared through the communication links between the individual organizations. When an organization receives the incoming information, the organization will transfer the requested resources or services to the requesting organization. If the organization does not supply the requested items, the organization will broadcast the information to its linked organizations.

To model this information processing behavior, we modeled the internal structure of the organization as Fig. 4.3. Particularly, we used the DEVS formalism (Ziegler et al. 2000) to describe our models in clear detail. We assumed that each organization had three information processing buffers and one decision-making model described in the following sections.

- Event Buffer: This buffer gathers the resource or service demands from its own organization. In the simulation, we fed such demands according to the communication records that we gathered. This buffer corresponds to the field unit of an organization that collects the relief demands.

Table 4.1 Summary of the Katrina dataset

Category	Descriptive statistics (over the period)
Number of events	2,227
Collection period	Aug. 27–Sep. 6 (264 h)
Involved Organizations	172
Exchanged services and resources	669
Number of communication links	2,303

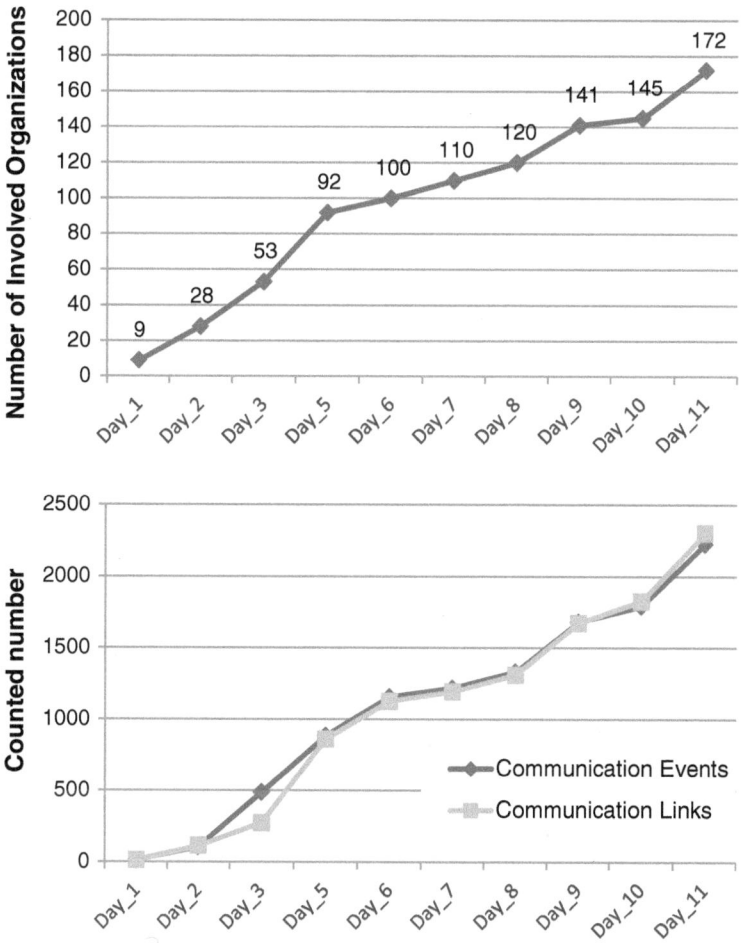

Fig. 4.2 (*Top*) Number of involved organizations over the period, (*Bottom*) Number of communication events and links between organizations over the period

- Broadcast Buffer: This buffer collects the broadcasted demand information from other organizations. Prior to the response decision or information relay decision, the received information is stored in the buffer. This buffer corresponds to the liaison unit of an organization that takes charge in communications.
- Response Buffer: This buffer collects the received resources or services from other organizations. Prior to the decision-maker's permission to deliver the received resources, the buffer stores the received items. This buffer corresponds to the logistical unit of an organization.
- Decision-making: Each organization has initial distributed resources and services that are at its disposal. (1) The decision-maker will respond and transfer the resources and the services to other organizations requesting them. (2) If the

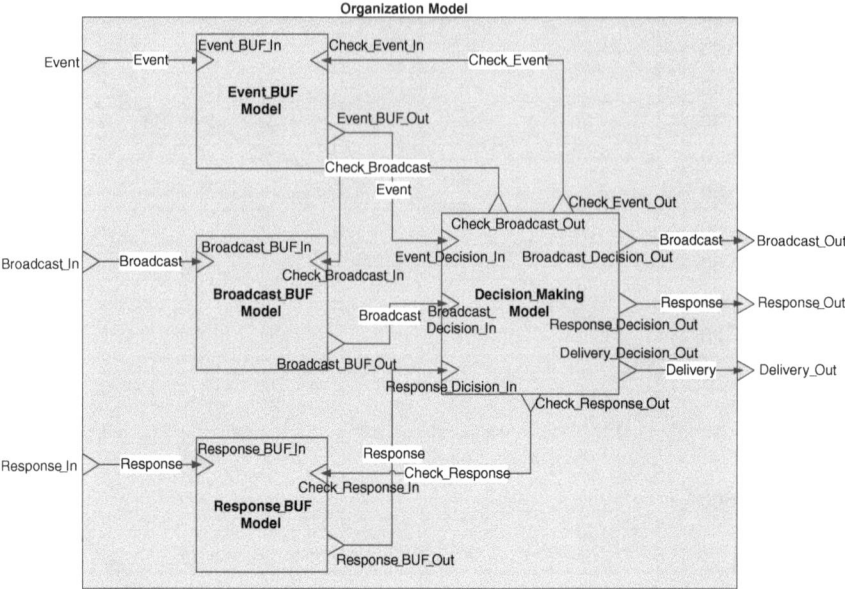

Fig. 4.3 Organization model's internal structure described in the DEVS coupled diagram. There are three information process buffer models and one decision-making model

organization does not have the requested resource or service, then the decision-maker will broadcast the requesting information to other linked organization. (3) Also, the decision-maker will confirm whether the requested item is delivered and used internally. (4) Otherwise, if a requested resource is delivered twice, then an over-delivered resource will be sent back by the decision-maker as a rejected response message.

The above behavior descriptions are more formally represented in the DEVS formalism in Figs. 4.4 and 4.5.

4.3.3 Interorganizational Structure

After modeling the intraorganizational structure of the relief organizations, we modeled the interorganizational structure as a collective of the organizations. According to the intraorganizational model in Figs. 4.6 and 4.7, the organizations exchange broadcast and response messages. The delivery message of an organization is used to count the successful resource transfer between organizations, so the particular message is not propagated to other organizations. We modeled that the broadcast messages were propagated through the established communication links between organizations which are recorded in the dataset. The established

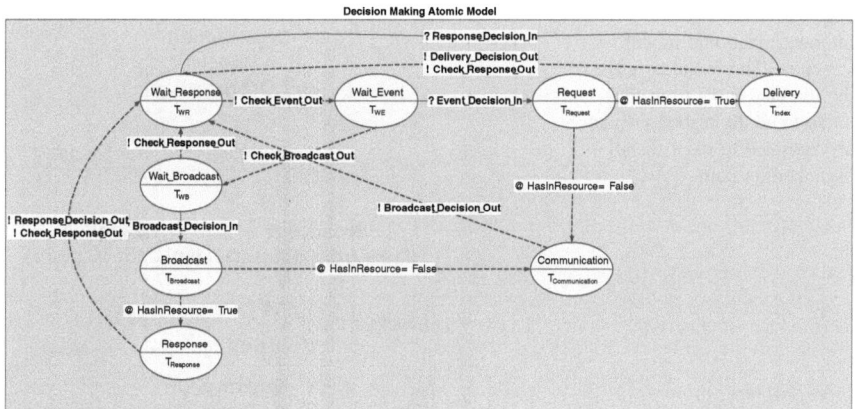

Fig. 4.4 Decision-making model's operational behavior described in the DEVS atomic diagram. The decision-making models determine when to send broadcast, response, and delivery messages

Fig. 4.5 Three buffer's operational behavior described in the DEVS atomic diagram

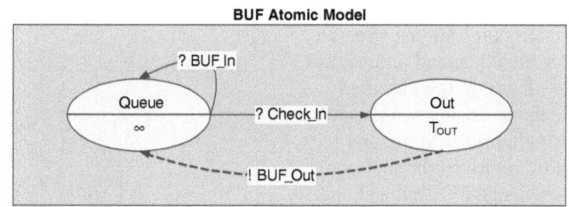

communication links increased from 13 links on day 1 to 2,303 links on day 11. These broadcast links were often unidirectional because some organizations were part of a hierarchical system that only submitted and took reports, according to the dataset.

Unlike the broadcast links that were gathered from the dataset, we assumed that the response links existed for all pairs of organizations because the responding organization must know the requesting organization since the broadcast message received by the responding organization specified which organization was requesting a specific resource.

Under this process, the message is the information of the resource request and also has time and organization sequences from request to response through the communication links to calculate the performance from a network-centric operation perspective.

4.3.4 Analysis from Network-Centric Operation Perspective

As we modeled the intra- and the inter-organizational structures of the crisis management, this case study aims at evaluating the performance of the collective

Fig. 4.6 A sample interorganizational model structure. The broadcasts are the directed links from the dataset and the response links are assumed to exist for all organization pairs

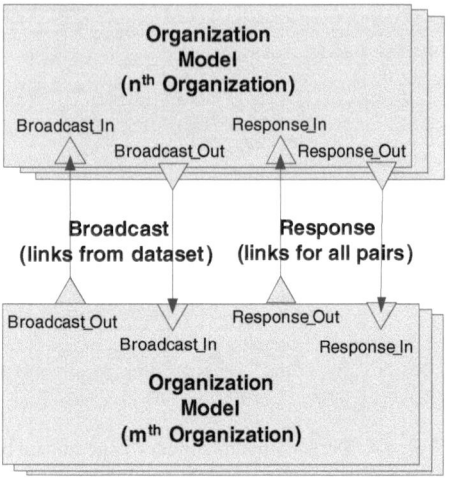

Fig. 4.7 The interorganizational structure, or the command and control structure in the observed dataset. Each *box* represents a single organization, and the link indicates the message exchange of command and control

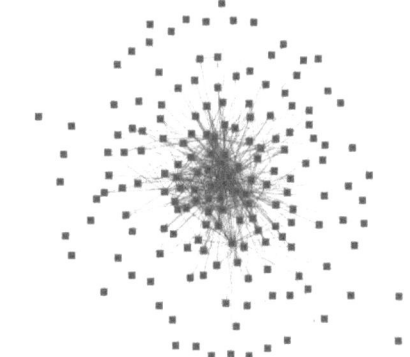

from the network-centric operations perspective. Alberts and Hayes claimed that the key to success in network-centric operations is the synchronized behavior of distributed organizations through well-developed shared situation awareness (Alberts and Hayes 2003). For instance, if one organization requires a certain resource, this demand information is expected to be rapidly shared across other organizations in the crisis management. This rapid situation sharing is captured as the increased shared situation awareness. Then, the organizations are expected to transfer the demanded resource to the demanding organization promptly without a specific command from authority. This self-motivated reaction is called self-synchronization in network-centric operations. Eventually, the successful network-centric operations of the increased shared situation awareness and the self-synchronized actions decrease the latency from the request to the response. To model this evaluation concept from the network-centric operations, we devised four performance indexes: delivered resource count (DRC), request–response latency (RRL), shared situation awareness (SSA), and failed synchronized actions (FSA).

4.3.4.1 Delivered Resource Count

We counted the number of requests that received responses successfully. Some requests were not satisfied if a link was not established to an organization possessing the requested resource.

4.3.4.2 Request–Response Latency

We measured the time delay in the simulation from the generation of the request to the reception of the response. This is a basic metric for measuring how long it would take to resolve a certain resource demand. We named the time delays the RRL. To calculate the RRL of an organization, we averaged the time delays for requests generated by an organization. To calculate the RRL of the interorganization, we averaged the RRL of the organizations.

4.3.4.3 Shared Situation Awareness

The SSA of an organization is measured as a ratio between the number of broadcast messages recognized by the organization and the total number of broadcast messages described in the below.

$$\text{messages}_i = \{m | m \in \text{broadcast buffer in organization}_i\}$$

$$\text{SSA}_i = \frac{n(\text{messages}_i)}{n(\bigcup_{j \in \text{organizations}} \text{messages}_j)}$$

The SSA of the interorganizational structure is the average of the SSA of the individual organizations.

$$\text{SSA} = \frac{\sum_{j \in \text{organizations}} \text{SSA}_j}{n(\text{organizations})}$$

4.3.4.4 Failed Synchronized Action

The FSA of an organization is the count of the over-delivery of the requested resources or services. If the broadcast is too widely propagated, the duplicated responses by multiple responding organizations to a single requesting organization could be over-reaction and under-utilization of the resources. This under-utilization of the resources due to uncoordinated responses is often observed in crisis management, and we measure this by FSA. Figure 4.8 describes the concept of this measure visually.

Fig. 4.8 Illustrative description of failed synchronized action and under-utilization of resources

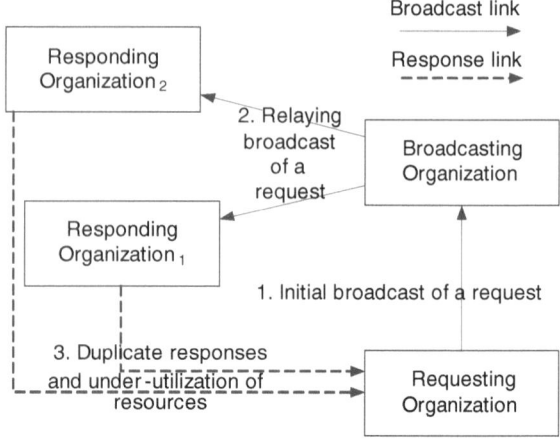

4.4 Virtual Experiment Design

Before we describe the virtual experiment design for simulations of the above model, we summarized the inputs, the outputs, and the parameters of the model in Table 4.2. Mainly, we varied the decision-making time delay because we focus on the information processing behavior of the intra- and the inter-organizations in a crisis. Also, we differentiated the established communication links by aggregating the links up to a specific date. This means we simulated the interorganizational structure established up to day i, and we change i from day 1 to day 11. These variations are also illustrated in Table 4.3. Since the model has stochastic time delays, each cell is repeatedly simulated 30 times.

4.5 Result

This section illustrates the virtual experiment results regarding the interorganizational performance from the network-centric operation perspectives.

4.5.1 Organizational Performance in Basic Metrics

The primary concern of this scenario is that the organizations operate as a well-organized interorganizational collective to deliver requested resources from one organization to another. Therefore, we measured on which day the interorganizational structure became mature and handled the resource requests effectively. Figure 4.9 describes the DRC under ten different interorganizational structures and three different decision-making speeds. Since this calculates the successful resource delivery without limiting the latency, the decision-making speed is not an

Table 4.2 Summary of model simulating the network-centric operations in the crisis

Type	Name	Value	Implication
Input	C2 Structure	Communication links up to a specific date in the dataset	Established communication link between organizations of the crisis management
	Scenario	Resource request records in the dataset	Resource demand record from organizations in the crisis period
Output	Failed synchronized action (FSA)	Measured from simulations	The count of duplicated responses and under-utilization of resources
	Shared situation awareness (SSA)	Measured from simulations	The ratio of shared broadcasted messages across organizations
	Request–response latency (RRL)	Measured from simulations	Time interval between a request and a response of a resource
	Delivered resource count (DRC)	Measured from simulations	Number of resources delivered as requested
Parameters	T-out in buffer model	Default = 0.1 (h)	Buffer's delay time in responding to the decision-making model's message checking
	T-wait in decision-making model	Default = 0.1 (h)	Decision-making model's delay time in message checking
	T-decision-making in decision-making model	Default = 1 (h) Slow = 2 (h) Fast = 0.5 (h)	The λ value of the Poisson distribution for the decision-making model's delay time in deciding whether a message should be rebroadcasted or responded by itself
	T-broadcast in decision-making model	Default = 0.1 (h) Slow = 0.2 (h) Fast = 0.05 (h)	The λ value of the Poisson distribution for the decision-making model's delay time in broadcasting the message to linked organizations
	T-response in decision-making model	Default = 1 (h) Slow = 2 (h) Fast = 0.5 (h)	The λ value of the Poisson distribution for the decision-making model's delay time in transferring the resources for responses
	T-delivery in decision-making model	Default = 1 (h) Slow = 2 (h) Fast = 0.5 (h)	The λ value of the Poisson distribution for the decision-making model's delay time in finishing the delivery of the resources internally

outstanding factor. On the other hand, the maturity of the interorganizational structure matters significantly. According to the trend of the DRC, 3 days of maturity were enough to reach the plateau of performance. Having said that, the successful deliveries were limited up to 903 requesting events, which was just 40.54 % of the generated requests. This means the interorganizational structure was not fully handling all the scenario events, and the structure stopped effective

Table 4.3 Summary of the virtual experimental design for testing the interorganizational structure from the network-centric operation perspective

Input parameters	Value	Implication
Interorganizational structure	Communication links up to a specific date in the dataset (10 cases)	Structure of communication links that was established and used for broadcasting information
T-decision-making, T-broadcast, T-response T-delivery	Default, slow, fast (3 cases)	Turn-around time for decision-making operations, or decision-making speeds
Total virtual experimental cells	30 cells (10 × 3 cases)	Each cell is replicated 30 times.

evolution on day 3. When we look at Fig. 4.10, the structure on day 3 had only 273 links out of 2,303 links in the whole period. Then, we conjectured whether the increased links may contribute to the fast responses for the generated requests. Figure 4.11 shows there was a certain decrease in the RRL, yet it was limited to 23.40 % of the decrease in latency. Also, it should be noted that the slow decision-making speed increased the latency about 2.57 times more than the latency from the default speed, while the slow decision-making speed was just 2 times slower than the default. This means broadcasts between organizations increased the latency more than linearly.

4.5.2 Organizational Performance in Network-Centric Operations

After observing the basic metrics of the organizational performance, we analyzed the organizational performances from the network-centric operation perspective. First, the shared situation awareness explained the limited DRCs. Figure 4.11 shows the shared situation awareness converged on day 5, the next day after day 3 in our dataset. The converged shared situation awareness value was about 0.03, indicating that an organization had three request information messages on average if there were a hundred distinct request information messages in the entire inter-organizational structure. Therefore, most organizations were not receiving the information messages properly and were not sharing the situation effectively.

Second, in Fig. 4.12, the count of the failed synchronized action, or the under-utilization of the resources, increased about 1.85 times when we compared the counts from day 3 to day 10. The increased links were used not in increasing the shared situation awareness, but in increasing the duplicated resource delivery. This result implies the increased links incrementally added to the established communication links on day 3 without careful consideration of the interorganizational structure as a whole.

Fig. 4.9 Delivered resource counts as the interorganizational matures throughout the period

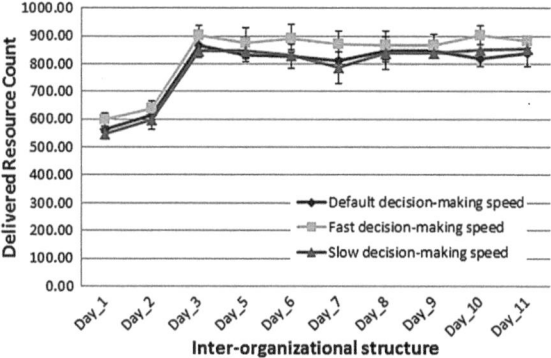

Fig. 4.10 Request–response latency as the interorganizational matures throughout the period

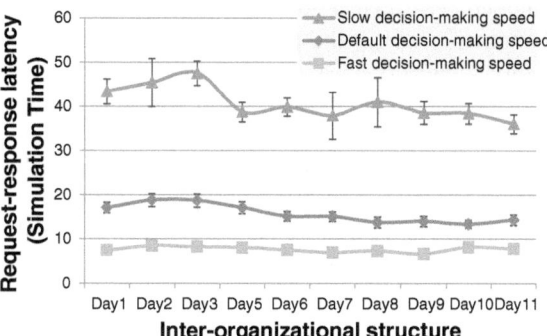

Fig. 4.11 Shared situation awareness as the interorganizational matures throughout the period

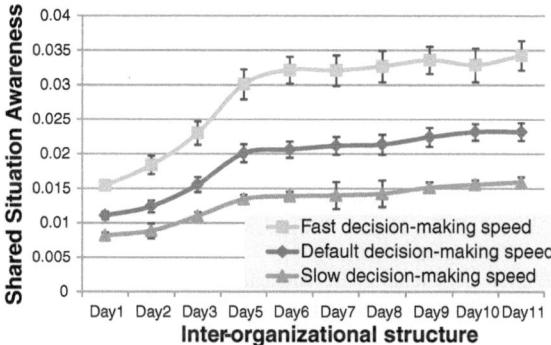

4.6 Lessons Learned to Model and Simulate Command and Control

This case study shows how to measure the performance of an organization and how the performance changes over-time. First, measuring organizational performance can be done at multiple levels. We may count the number of tasks completed, which is a simple and naïve measurement. Further, we may measure the

Fig. 4.12 Failed
synchronized action, or
duplicated resource delivery,
as the interorganizational
matures throughout the
period

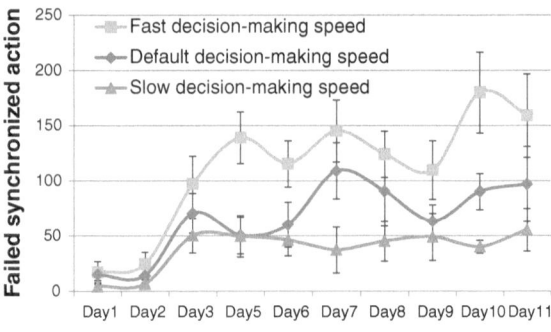

implicit performance, such as shared situation awareness to gauge the information congruence across the participants in command and control. Second, the organizational performance does not always increase as the command and control structure gets complicated. From this case study, we expected that the organizational performance to be more mature as the situation progresses. However, from the simulation result, we observed that the organizational performance increases to a limited extent even though the command and control structure becomes denser. This might be caused by the information overload, and this means that agents are not sending information to the ones that can handle their requests. Rather, the agents seem to be just broadcasting the information to the general channel, and this is causing the information overload. This suggests that the design of command and control structure should be sufficient enough to handle critical information as well as be succinct to reduce any delays in the command and control procedure.

References

Alberts, D.S., Hayes, R.E.: Power to the Edge: Command and Control in the Information Age. DoD CCRP, Washington (2003)

Alberts, D.S., Hayes, R.E.: Understanding Command and Control. DOD, CCRP Press, Washington (2006)

Beavan, J., Fielding, E., Motagh, M., Samsonov, S., Donnelly, N.: Fault location and slip distribution of the 22 February 2011 Mw 6.2 Christchurch, New Zealand, earthquake from geodetic data. Seismol. Res. Lett. **82**(6), 789–799 (2011)

Bharosa, N., Lee, J., Janssen, M.: Challenges and obstacles in sharing and coordinating information during multi-agency disaster response: Propositions from field exercises. Inf. Syst. Front. **12**(1), 49–65 (2009)

Comfort, L.K.: Inter-organizational design for disaster management: cognition, commu-nication, coordination, and control. JSEE: Spring Summer **9**(1), 61–71 (2007)

Comfort, L.K., Oh, N., Ertan, G., Scheinert, S.: Designing adaptive systems for disaster mitigation and response: The role of structure. In: Designing Resilience: Preparing for Ex-treme Events, 1st ed. Universuty of Pittsburgh Press, (2010)

Lee, G., Jung, K.: Analysis of flood and landslide due to torrential rain in Seoul, Korea on July, 2011. Proceedings of the Korean Society for Industrial and Applied Mathematics **6**(2), pp. 47–48 (2011)

Lee, G., Oh, N., Moon, I.C.: Modeling and Simulating Network-Centric Operations of Organizations for Crisis Management, SpringSim' 2012, Orlando, Florida, 26–29 March 2012

Matanle, P.: The Great East Japan Earthquake, tsunami, and nuclear meltdown: towards the (re)construction of a safe, sustainable, and compassionate society in Japan's shrinking regions. Local Environ. **16**(9), 823–847 (2011)

Moffat, J.: The Response to Hurricane Katrina: A Case Study of Changing C2 Maturity. DoD CCRP, Washington (2008)

Oh, N., Moon, I.C.: Searching new structure for effective resource distribution in the disaster management system—multi agent simulation approach. In: 69th ASPA Annual Conference, pp. 1–19 (2008)

Oomes, A.H.J.: Organization awareness in crisis management: Dynamic organigrams for more effective disaster response. In: ISCRAM2004, pp. 63–68, (2004)

Quijada, S.E.: A Hybrid Simulation Methodology to Evaluate Network Centric Decision Making under Extreme Events. University of Central Florida, Orlando (2006)

Rosen, J., et al.: The future of command and control for disaster response. IEEE Eng. Med. Biol. Mag. **21**(5), 56–68 (2002)

Schultz, C.H., Koenig, K.L., Noji, E.K.: A medical disaster response to reduce immediate mortality after an earthquake. N. Engl. J. Med. **334**(7), 438–444, (1996)

Smith, D.M.: A Study of Command and Control of Multi-Agency Disaster Response Operations. University of Phoenix, Phoenix (2010)

von Lubitz, D.K.J.E., Beakley, J.E., Patricelli, F.: Disaster management: the structure, function, and significance of network-centric operations. J. Homel. Secur. Emerg. Manag. **5**(1) (2008)

Waugh, W.L., Streib, G.: Collaboration and leadership for effective emergency management. Pub. Adm. Rev. **66**(1), 131–140 (2006)

Ziegler, B.P., Herbert, P., Kim, T.G.: Theory of Modeling and Simulation, 2 edn. Academic Press, New York (2000)

Chapter 5
Conclusion

This book presented three case studies of command and control. The first case study was modeling and simulating command and control of a terror organization for terror missions. These case studies are different in the analyzed domain as well as the approach of modeling and simulation. The distinct approach of the first case study was modeling multiple command and control structure spaces that were social space and geospace. The case study demonstrated the command and control structure in the social dimension influence the changes of the command and control structure in the geospatial dimension, and vice versa. So far, many models of command and control focused on a single dimension where the command and control structure rests in. For instance, many studied the organizational chart to see the command hierarchy by discussing the length of chain of commands as well as the number of subordinate units under a single command. However, this case study argues that such studies might be limited in providing valuable insights when the analyzed force is deployed to the actual operational environment. When a force is deployed to the field, the operational environment, such as geospatial distance and terrain, would heavily influence the command and control structure in the organizational chart.

- Lesson 1: Modeling and simulating command and control should cover the features of operational environment of interests. The operational environment can be a joint space of multiple dimensions, such as social, geospatial, temporal, cyber, etc. Modelers should remember that the command and control structure rest in the multiple dimensions. The command and control structure viewed from one dimension may influence the same structure represented in another dimension, and this should be reflected to the model.

The second case study was modeling and simulating command and control of a military organization for naval air defense. The uniqueness of the second case study was interoperating the models of different levels of command and control which were the mission level and the engagement level. When we consider command and control as the top commander's decision-making and order propagation, this is misguided in the recent combats. Each participating unit in the

I.-C. Moon et al., *Modeling and Simulating Command and Control*,
SpringerBriefs in Computer Science, DOI: 10.1007/978-1-4471-5037-4_5,
© Il-Chul Moon 2013

command and control structure has its own commanding officer, and the commanding officer has own command and control scope and responsibility. However, the view at the mission level command and control would be different from the view at the engagement level command and control. This would lead to different modeling and simulation focuses on command and control. The mission-level model would be interested in the mission execution and its corresponding command and control activities. The engagement-level model might concentrate on how to increase the survival ratio of friendlies and the kill ratio of adversaries. Traditionally, these two different command and control foci were handled by two different models, and this is why we have differentiated the modeling scope of models. However, our case study shows that focusing just single level of command and control would produce a different result from modeling multiple levels of command and control. For example, our result indicates that faster decision making would be always preferable when using only the mission-level model, but when we interoperate the mission-level model and the engagement-level model, we found that there is a right length of decision-making cycle that gives enough time to observe evolving engagement situation.

- Lesson 2: Modeling and simulating command and control should consider its multiple levels. Command and control may happen at the theater, mission, and engagement levels in the combat situation. Each level has its unique objective to accomplish, and the objectives might not be aligned in the same direction in the situation. Hence, modelers should consider the interaction of commanders and units in the horizontal aspect as well as the vertical aspect of the command and control structure.

The final case study was modeling and simulating command and control of civil organizations for disaster response. This case study presents multiple organizational performance measures that are drawn from the information domain, the physical domain, and the cognitive domain. The measures include the resource delivery count, the delivery latency, the degree of shared situation awareness, and the count of failed synchronized actions. Typical models measure the organizational performance by achieving objectives of command and control. While measuring the performance by the objectives is the baseline measure, we need to develop measures to see the implicit performance of command and control. A force may achieve its goal though it may not share the information well across the commanders and the units. Further, our case study demonstrates using a simple network statistics to measure the performance of the structure is doubtable. Our case study indicates that the dense command and control structure which should be the indicator of better cooperation across commanders and units actually increases the information overload and eventually limit the entire organizational performance. Measuring the performance of the network structure should be done by jointly using network analysis as well as simulation analysis because the network analysis on a snapshot structure would not provide the dynamic nature of the command and control procedure.

- Lesson 3: Modeling and simulating command and control should develop explicit and implicit organizational performance measures. Measuring the performance by the objectives is just the baseline analysis. Modelers should consider measuring the implicit organizational performance, i.e., shared situation awareness and synchronized action, in the information, cognition, and physical domains. Simple measures on structure would be intuitive to interpret, yet such measures might disguise the actual performance if the analysis is not accompanied by the intensive analysis on the dynamic nature of the structure.

This book concludes with the above three lessons learned from our three case studies in the intelligence, military, and disaster management domains. Designing command and control is a difficult task given command and control actually takes place in an extreme situation that is urgent, risky, and uncertain. Many researches ignore such situational factors and simplify them because such factors are often difficult to model. However, our findings suggest that the essence of modeling and simulating command and control lies in those difficult factors to model. We expect that the future modeling and simulation of command and control would be more situated in the context of operational environment and operating organization.